PRAISE FOR

Racism, Hypocrisy, and Bad Faith:

A Moral Challenge to the America I Love

"Julius Bailey is one of the most original and courageous philosophers of his generation. In this powerful text, we once again see his unique ability to wed his sharp analysis and philosophical acumen to our American contemporary crises!"
—CORNEL WEST, Professor of the Practice of Public Philosophy, Harvard University, author of *Race Matters*

"*Racism, Hypocrisy, and Bad Faith: A Moral Challenge to the America I Love* is the prophetic thunder that is needed in such a time as this. The book is meant to convict and convert us to a higher moral standard grounded in truth and justice, instead of hypocrisy and bad faith."
—ANDRE E. JOHNSON, The University of Memphis

"Dr. Bailey offers a sophisticated understanding of our current socio-political climate and the structural realities that inhibit efforts to advance equity and inclusion. He eloquently reminds us of our moral responsibility to align values and actions, resist racist policies that perpetuate inequality, and demand that leaders be held accountable for their actions. His aspirational vision for a civil, multiracial democracy is built on a commitment to search for truth as well as authentic engagement with others recognizing the promise of intersectionality in building powerful communities of hope. This vision is heartening for those of good will who value the powerful ties that bind us together in the common endeavor of finally delivering on America's promise of freedom, opportunity, equality, and justice for all."
—LAURIE M. JOYNER, President, Saint Xavier University

"*Racism, Hypocrisy, and Bad Faith* is passionate and well written. It is a timely and well-researched scholarly evaluation of current events. The book asks readers to question how we as a nation are living up to the promises that are vital to the American experiment, including the promise to continually improve."
—BISHOP SUZANNE DARCY DILLAHUNT, Southern Ohio Synod, Evangelical Lutheran Church in America

"Julius Bailey has written a timely book. With philosophical nuance and a clear focus on the practical challenges we face in the Age of Trump, Bailey demonstrates how bad faith corrodes democratic life in this country. He writes with passion and insight. He looks the darkness of the hour squarely in the face and still holds a hope that we can 'tear down the edifices of hypocrisy and bad faith and replace them with edifices of truth ... and good faith.' I needed to read this book!"
—EDDIE S. GLAUDE, James S. McDonnell Distinguished University Professor, Princeton University

"In *Racism, Hypocrisy, and Bad Faith*, Professor Julius Bailey presents an extremely timely discussion of the temperament of today's politics during the post-Obama years—effectively known as 'the Trump era.' Through accounts of various examples of 'bad faith,' Bailey establishes the existence of a corrupt form of politics that veers away from principles of integrity and earnestness toward the public good. In bad faith, the singular interests of politicians take center stage under the guise of gas-lighted information that hides the course of political actions that are actually hypocritical and ill-formed. Through examination of several race-related political issues, Bailey provides examples of bad-faith politics that disingenuously promote one face of a political issue while providing voice and support for another. As Bailey suggests, 'dog whistles' unite the ears of those supporting bad-faith actions. Sincerity and genuineness go unnoticed, until transparency introduces truth in the face of majority rule and popular sovereignty, bringing an interest in good-faith politics to the fore. By deconstructing examples from different contexts and times, Bailey shows how bad faith is an undue (and, hopefully, mutable) disruption of democracy."
—SHAYLA C. NUNNALLY, University of Connecticut

RACISM, HYPOCRISY,

AND

BAD FAITH

RACISM, HYPOCRISY,

AND

BAD FAITH

A Moral Challenge to the America I Love

JULIUS BAILEY

broadview press

BROADVIEW PRESS — www.broadviewpress.com
Peterborough, Ontario, Canada

Founded in 1985, Broadview Press remains a wholly independent publishing house.
Broadview's focus is on academic publishing; our titles are accessible to university and college
students as well as scholars and general readers. With 800 titles in print, Broadview has
become a leading international publisher in the humanities, with world-wide distribution.
Broadview is committed to environmentally responsible publishing and fair business practices.

Library and Archives Canada Cataloguing in Publication

Title: Racism, hypocrisy, and bad faith : a moral challenge to the America I love /
    Julius Bailey.
Names: Bailey, Julius, 1970- author.
Description: Includes bibliographical references.
Identifiers: Canadiana (print) 20200169904 | Canadiana (ebook) 20200169955 | ISBN
    9781554814985 (softcover) | ISBN 9781770487376 (PDF) | ISBN 9781460406939 (HTML)
Subjects: LCSH: United States—Moral conditions. | LCSH: Political culture—United
    States. | LCSH: United States—Politics and government—2017- | LCSH: United States—
    Social conditions—21st century. | LCSH: United States—Race relations.
Classification: LCC E169.12 .B35 2020 | DDC 973.933—dc23

Broadview Press handles its own distribution in North America:
PO Box 1243, Peterborough, Ontario K9J 7H5, Canada
555 Riverwalk Parkway, Tonawanda, NY 14150, USA
Tel: (705) 743-8990; Fax: (705) 743-8353
email: customerservice@broadviewpress.com

For all territories outside of North America, distribution is handled by Eurospan Group.

Canada

Broadview Press acknowledges the financial support of the Government of Canada for our
publishing activities.

Edited by Martin R. Boyne
Book design by Michel Vrana

PRINTED IN CANADA

To those whose desire for equality instills daily agitation.

CONTENTS

CONTENTS

PREFACE

AS WE CLOSED IN ON THE MIDNIGHT HOUR ON ELEC-
tion night, it was becoming clearer with each passing moment that
we were on the verge of entering a new era in American politics. The
campaign had been unlike any before it but buoyed by polls showing
Hillary Clinton as the odds-on favorite to emerge from the campaign
bruised but victorious, and we were quite sure that there would be
some return to normalcy. As the results came in, though, we started
to see that our optimism had been misplaced. Donald Trump had
taken the key battleground states Ohio (a bellwether for every presidential election since 1964) and Florida. Within a matter of hours, he
crossed the 270-electoral-vote threshold, guaranteeing that he would
become the forty-fifth president of the United States.

Even before the clocks on the east coast were striking twelve, the
scapegoating had begun. Hillary's failings as a candidate stood out
as the most obvious reason for Trump's victory. Her message did not

resonate with voters in crucial swing states, and, while the left was animated by anti-Trump animus, it was not united. Bernie-boosting progressives had been severely disappointed with the primary results, and some said they would rather stay home on election night than hold their noses while marking an X on the ballot. Though they viewed Hillary in a more flattering light than Trump, they described her as the lesser of two evils—evidence of a severe dearth of the kind of enthusiasm necessary to drive liberal voters to the polls in overwhelming numbers.

Young liberals wanted a candidate that could inspire them the way that Obama had inspired voters in 2008. Litmus tests and our search for a hero worthy of our worship made it nearly impossible to cohere around a single candidate. Rather than searching for somebody who was electable, we on the left were searching for a progressive savior. Obama was a candidate and then a president who took office freighted with the messianic hopes of legions of progressive voters. He was a cult hero, a man who represented the turning of a page in American history. We on the left expected the next candidate to represent a further and even-more-aggressive movement toward the utopian horizon. An establishment candidate like Hillary didn't align (at least not neatly) with progressive hopes, and this opened the door to a very different kind of candidate—one who promised to be a savior of a very different sort.

On the right, voters were cohering around a candidate as flawed as any who has run for public office. Trump should never have been on the ballot in the first place, but he ran roughshod over the primaries precisely because the GOP was either unequipped or unwilling (most likely a combination of the two) to do anything about a candidate who openly flaunted democratic norms, made explicitly autocratic promises, and traded in bad-faith arguments and conspiracy theories. They had been priming the party for a candidate like Trump since the Tea Party rallies during Obama's first term. At Trump's rallies, like the Tea Party rallies but on a larger and more horrifying scale, the GOP was pulled steadily from bad to worse and from worse to worst, with Trump promising quite literally *anything* that came in the form of an applause line. Though there was a smattering of early principled resistance from within the party, the party leadership quickly fell into line, shrugging their shoulders at each new outrage. Trump called on foreign adversaries for assistance, he threatened to lock up his political opponent, he disrespected a war hero[1] (a much-esteemed member of his party no less), and he insulted a Gold-Star family,[2] and senior members of the party looked the other way or twisted themselves into knots trying to excuse their party's candidate.

Now, the GOP and I have very rarely agreed during my lifetime, but I can remember a Republican party that was dignified and steadfast in its values. I may not have agreed with those values, but they held them sincerely and could usually defend their position intelligently. The GOP candidates that I can remember—Reagan, Bush Sr. and Jr., Bob Dole, Newt Gingrich, John McCain—had very different visions for America than my own, but they *had* a vision for America. They wanted to make this country better. Some may have been corrupt and self-indulgent, but not to their core; they may have enjoyed the attention that the office brought with it, but that attention was a by-product of their role as the nation's top civil servant. Their campaigns were extensions of their political wills and philosophies, not of their tawdry personal brands. They saw themselves as servants of America's democracy, as protectors of its values and its people. As a candidate, Trump may have hugged flags publicly and crowed about his unsurpassed love of country, but this was transparent political theater, with the flag as prop. He loves himself (not his country) to the point of obsession. With a man like Trump at its helm, the GOP has given away every shred of its credibility as a party of principles and family values. It is now openly, transparently hypocritical, a grisly political machine that is slowly grinding our democracy to dust. Forced to choose between party and country, GOP leaders have overwhelmingly chosen the former, lying brazenly to defend their leader and his band of sinister incompetents.

Perhaps most troublingly, the GOP has all but openly embraced the courting of white nationalists and white supremacists, who grew bolder with each dog-whistle rally. Trump had them to thank for his rise through the primaries, and the GOP seems, now, to accept its bedfellows with open arms, happy to continue to lower the baseline of the acceptable with no seeming limits to how low it might go. The party's feet are now planted firmly on a foundation of racism and revanchism, and there's no easy way for them to extricate themselves from the muck. The baseline of the acceptable has been in freefall since Trump announced his candidacy in 2015, and the party has effectively hitched its buggy to this horse. The party may have, for a time, been attempting to modernize and shed the widespread perception that it is the party of old white men, but now it is leaning into this—and leaning hard. Deplorables once pushed to the margins of the party were now whispering in the president's ear and defending him on television. Trump was, they said, the cure for what ailed America—the only leader willing to turn his back to the horizon and, dragging the country behind him, march back in the direction from which we had come.

And backward march is exactly what he has done. Rolling back as much of Obama's progressive legacy as he can, and stacking the courts with deeply conservative justices who may soon give the evangelicals who threw their support behind Trump (even though his philandering and corruption should have turned their collective stomach) exactly what they have long sought: a state-by-state overturning of *Roe v. Wade*.[3] Trump promised to make America great again, and he is hard at work making Obama's America look more like Reagan's or even Nixon's.

With each stroke of Trump's felt-tipped pen, we are pulled further and further from the multi-racial democracy that we—for the briefest of moments—believed might be possible. What's more, we are pulled further and further from the kind of democracy envisioned by our Founding Fathers. The democracy they outlined in the founding documents represented a quick and decisive movement away from the kings, queens, and emperors of Europe. They placed limits on the power of the individual to entirely upend the country and the lives of those within its borders. No man or woman was to be granted God-like powers—indeed, even God himself was kept off to one side. The *demos*, the citizenry, was to be protected from even its elected rulers, who might, after all, prove themselves far less responsible than appearances first suggested. We knew, from the outset, that the fallacy of divine-right kingship had no place in an effective democracy, and on these grounds, America was to be different.

The office of the presidency was to be an honor bestowed on the deserving. The office was to be kept in check, with the sum of the government's constitutive parts far outweighing the authority of the president. The founding premise of this office's establishment was that even the best among us cannot be trusted to rule without built-in intermediaries and checks and balances. Our leaders are not to be seen as or, indeed, to present themselves as saviors, but that's exactly what we've asked them to be. Our messianic political hopes opened the door for one (like Trump) who claims to be the only one who can fix an utterly broken system. Only he—not us, and not our democracy—can save us.

We long for a take-no-prisoners single leader, and, on both left and right, this means we have introduced problematic elements into our democracy. On the right, there is the longing for the strong arm of the autocrat; on the left, the need for the perfect or nearly perfect politician and the concomitant breath holding and feet stamping when the candidate of our choice doesn't advance to the final round. Since one of these drives voters to the polls and the other keeps them at home, is it any surprise that the right holds not just the Oval Office but also the balance of power in the Senate and in so many state legislatures?

We on the left are already priming ourselves for another disappointment in 2020. Even if we manage to remove Trump from office, the balance of legislative power may well still be in the hands of Republicans. To make good on their surely lofty promises, the next Democrat to hold the office—assuming they must reckon with a stonewalling Congress—may feel entitled to further erode the democratic institutions that have suffered so mightily under Trump. This is where our messianic hopes lead—to an uprooted democracy that can be bent to suit the whims of whatever mandate-granted populist sits behind the Resolute Desk; to a pinballing escalation of the culture-war quagmire we've found ourselves in; to an America that drifts yet further from the civil, multi-racial democracy that we might yet become.

We are a divided nation longing to become whole. We can find some semblance of civility and progress, but only if we learn to recognize and root out bad-faith arguments and hypocrisy—cancers that have taken root at the heart of our political discourse. Though these may currently be the GOP's stock in trade, progressives too have placed political expediency before the unvarnished truth. If progressives are to be the ones who restore some sense of normalcy in Washington, they must show the American public that we've reached the end of this bitter and hyper-partisan chapter in American history.

We must plant our feet on the truth, must make our stock in trade straight dealing and good faith. We must show the GOP that trust in our democracy and our institutions is more politically powerful than distrust of the same, must show them that faith is more powerful than cynicism. By doing so, we might effect a change in both parties, might return, not to complete agreement, but at least to a civilized form of political disagreement. We might never be of one mind, but we might yet be one sound political body.

Notes

1   Referring to the late Senator John McCain, when Trump said on 18 July 2015, at a Family Leadership Summit in Ames, Iowa, "He's not a war hero.... He was a war hero because he was captured. I like people who weren't captured."

2   Khizr and Ghazala Khan's son, Humayun Khan, was killed during Operation Iraqi Freedom in 2004. Trump was on a tirade about banning Muslims, and Mr. Khan, at the Democratic National Convention of 2016, affirmed both his and his son's allegiance to America by picking up a pocket version of the US Constitution. Trump retaliated by asking whether his wife didn't speak because Muslims don't allow women to.

3   Many states are passing abortion laws that challenge the Supreme Court's standing. With Alabama and Georgia being the most restrictive, other states like Ohio, Kentucky, and Indiana have also passed these restrictive laws. At the time of this writing, only New York and Vermont have passed laws protecting against any *Roe v. Wade* alteration.

ACKNOWLEDGMENTS

TO MY IMMEDIATE FAMILY—SANDRA, BIANCA, HEATHER, AND JASMINE—THANK YOU FOR LOVING ME.

To Matt Bewig, Douglas Matus, Stephanie Bosco-Ruggerio, and Bryan Szabo, who all, in your own way, carefully push me to be a better writer, thinker, and facilitator of ideas.

To my fine Wittenberg University family, who remain consistent in their support for a troublemaker like me. I acknowledge the project grant from the Faculty Development Fund Board, and I appreciate the many student comments and engagements both in and out of class, especially my fall 2017 First Year Seminar students. Both in class and every week since, you have endured my ranting, my frustration, while simultaneously being by my side. Many of you have helped me shape the ideas found in this important book. To my university president, Michael Frandsen, and former provost, Mary Jo Zembar, who gave me unobstructed time, in the summer of 2019, to labor in this project. Drs. J. Robert Baker and Nancy McHugh, thank you for your generosity of time and intellectual talent pushing me in the right directions.

Very special thanks go to my *Degreed Money Entertainment Family* (ShaDawn Battle, Dalitso Ruwe, A.D. Carson, and Karlos Marshall), my brother Ray Jones, my sisters Zori Parker, Janice Williams, Robin Hill, Lisa and Letrisa Jones. To my friend and co-parent, Monica, thank you for bearing the weight. Shout out to Yvonka Hall and the entire Northeast Ohio Black Health Coalition family for your unwavering support and trust in me.

Dr. Rick Incorvati and Kent Brooks, when you created the summer 2019 "On Becoming Beloved Community" series, you reminded me of the purpose for this book, and I am glad to witness your work in the Springfield community and Ohio proper.

Last, but certainly not least, a heartfelt appreciation is extended to everyone at Broadview Press. Thank you for entering this journey again with me.

Introduction

INDEFENSIBLE MORALITY

American Conservative Duplicity in the
Era of Trump

I am strongly in favor of common sense, common honesty and common
decency. This makes me forever ineligible to any public office of trust or
profit in the Republic.
—*H.L. Mencken*

AT THE MEMORIAL SERVICE FOR OFFICERS SLAIN IN
the 2016 Dallas police massacre, George W. Bush salvaged his political
legacy by doing something usually considered unpresidential: he
rebuked a sitting president. "We have seen our discourse degraded by
casual cruelty," he said. "Too often, we judge other groups by their
worst examples while judging ourselves by our best intentions."[1] After
delivering his speech, Bush calmly returned to his seat and shared a
handshake and heartfelt embrace with Barack Obama. This display
of decency—the call for honorable discourse, the display of bipartisan
consensus—did more than put Bush back on the right side of history.

It also reminded the American people—especially those who voted for Bush just twelve years earlier—of their civic responsibilities, as well as how far their standards had slipped. Who could ever imagine such a display of integrity from Donald Trump?

The election of Trump signaled the triumph of hypocrisy over integrity—of judging others by their worst examples while judging ourselves by our best intentions. Bad-faith arguments have poisoned the well of civic discourse. Flagrant corruption and nepotism have shifted the goalposts of the acceptable so far that we are no longer on a recognizable playing field. How can we ask for or even demand political engagement when democratic norms are being flouted every day? How can we look this generation of new voters in the eye and tell them that tomorrow will be better, when each news cycle brings with it fresh outrages and new lows? Won't they blame us for our seeming inability to reverse course? Tomorrow's challenges may make today's seem almost surmountable by comparison. What are we doing to shore up the systems and institutions that tomorrow's Americans will depend on to help them weather the coming storm? How long can we hold out if the pendulum swings further to the right? Will our country survive an eight-year Trump presidency? On the morning after Bush Jr. was re-elected in 2004, the *Daily Mirror*, a left-leaning British newspaper, ran the headline "How can 59,054,087 people be so DUMB?" Imagine the headlines around the world if, after four years of being gaslighted every day by our current president, we sign up for another four.

In order to prevent this happening, we need to understand how we got here, and we need to know who is to blame—but endless debates over culpability are not only distracting us from solving the structural insecurities in our political system; they are also rewarding bad actors by amplifying their deliberate attempts to sow discord. We as a nation have a reckoning ahead of us—a reckoning of the scarred political landscape and of our roles in abandoning our responsibilities as citizens to hold corrupt politicians in check. Such a reckoning may not be possible while we are merely reacting to a news cycle dominated and controlled by the president and his disinformation campaign. So it goes that Democrats are outraged by one of Trump's outrageous tweets; Republicans respond by bringing up Barack Obama's "bitter clingers" remark or Hillary's "basket of deplorables." Trump brings out the worst in all of us simply by getting our attention, by distracting us from managing our own problems and forcing us to share in his distorted, amoral reality in which integrity is a myth and anyone claiming to possess it is a liar. This "whataboutism" leaves us powerless against corrupt politicians and foreign governments who seek to sabotage the state by eroding the public's trust in its institutions. This is the reality that Bush warned against in his 2016 memorial speech: a reality characterized by a disparity between our principles and our actions; a world of weaponized hypocrisy.

Hypocrisy is best understood as a contradiction between an individual's moral commitment and their actions. A "moral commitment" is an articulated belief or moral position; such commitments are ubiquitous in public life, though some are more visible than others. For instance, a position paper on a politician's web page might make it clear that they believe that *abortion is wrong*. Similarly, a citizen attending a pro-choice rally implies by their presence that they believe *banning abortion* is wrong. Hypocrisy means acting in a way that violates a moral commitment: the pro-life politician who gets an abortion is a hypocrite; the pro-choice citizen who condemns a friend for getting an abortion is a hypocrite. Hypocrisy applies different standards to different people; it condones or condemns based not on principle but on context.

Accusations of hypocrisy abound in the media today and are not limited to either side of the political aisle. Representative Scott Desjarlais (R-Tenn) advertised his pro-life stance on his web page, yet this obvious moral commitment did not stop him from urging his mistress to seek an abortion when political expedience—his self-interest—required it.[2] Joe Biden made sexual harassment a central issue during his time as vice-president, and he "rewrote the book" on sex and consent on college campuses during the Obama administration, emphasizing a policy of little or no tolerance and the imperative to obtain consent before physical contact.[3] A moral commitment could not be plainer, yet this commitment did not prevent Biden from touching multiple women without their consent—including a young college student at an event about the issue of sexual violence on campus.[4]

Politicians are naturally more susceptible to accusations of hypocrisy, not only because running for president usually involves an extraordinary level of public scrutiny but also because they are compelled to adopt political positions that both accord with their individual identity *and* do not contradict the core values of their party. Yet politicians are also more likely to gain, at least in the short term, from committing conscious acts of political hypocrisy. To take a moral stance is not just to endorse a position; it is to announce one's support for punishment of those who violate the rule. When people violate moral rules, the group—or the state—has license to punish them. Politicians who accept hypocrisy as a necessary evil are more likely to weaponize their moral commitments against their political opponents while applying different ethical boundaries to members of their own party. It has become commonplace to refer to such individuals, who either feign ignorance of their double standards or delude themselves into believing their integrity is intact, as "bad faith" actors.

In the era of Trump, the term "bad faith" has become a ubiquitous descriptor of what John Herrman at the *New York Times* has called a political moment marked by "mendacity and duplicitousness and engineered confusion."[5] The hypocrisies of the Trump administration are so extensive, and accusations of "bad faith" so frequent, that the term may be losing its clout. As Herrman observes, "Shouting 'bad faith' can sound like shouting 'no fair'—and revealing your previously undisturbed expectation that you will always be treated fairly." It is true that the term's modern usage has been impoverished through overuse, and that, as Megan Garber has argued in *The Atlantic*, its meaning has become "conveniently expansive and conveniently specific."[6] But if the ubiquitous modern usage of the term has deprived it of its accusatory power, the philosophical concept of bad faith remains unquestionably and profoundly relevant to the current moment's many political hypocrisies and raises important questions about how we might more productively call them out.

Bad faith is best understood as a form of hypocrisy, or as an absence of integrity. Whereas an individual who demonstrates integrity does so by acting according to their principles, an individual who demonstrates hypocrisy knowingly or unknowingly acts in a way that contradicts or undermines their principles. The question of whether individuals knowingly or unknowingly contradict themselves is central to Jean-Paul Sartre's definition of bad faith. According to Sartre, an individual becomes a bad faith actor when they use free will to deny their free will. Acting in bad faith, then, involves self-denial: it is a performative relinquishing of agency that is itself an act of individual agency, a submission to a social order that contradicts the self, and thus an essential hypocrisy.

Yet if the "bad faith" actors that dominate the news and social media do not appear to lack agency, this is because bad faith does not limit but rather enables the individual to act in ways in which a person of integrity would not. Moreover, deception is most successful when it is carried out with the appearance of conviction; and what better way to appear convinced of something than to convince oneself? The philosopher David Detmer cautions that Sartre's understanding of the bad faith actor should be carefully distinguished from that of the cynic, who operates with complete awareness of their actions. Detmer suggests that bad faith is "in many ways a superior strategy" to cynicism because it is more persuasive: "I will probably be more convincing, more believable, if I am perceived to believe what I am saying than if I am not so perceived; and I will be more likely to be so perceived if I truly do believe what I am saying."[7] If we apply this logic to the 2016 election, we might say that Hillary Clinton, believed by many to be a person of integrity as well as a cynic, was confined to telling the truth or lying unconvincingly; whereas Trump, in affirming whichever principles, values, or narrative most appealed to his audience, was granted a freedom that Clinton, in remaining true to herself and to her image, manifestly lacked.

If Sartre's understanding of bad faith helps us make sense of the freedoms granted by the Trump administration's flexible moral code, it also points to a more significant flaw in the US political system: namely, the lack of an effective standard or enforceable measure for political integrity that does not involve taking an oath. Without integrity, which they are not legally required to demonstrate unless speaking under oath, politicians are more likely to produce and support policies based on arguments that are in conflict with their public political positions. They become bad faith actors when they relinquish their agency in favor of political conformity. Their performance of self-denial is more effective than integrity—at least in the short term—because it grants them maneuverability and power.

Though no language in the Constitution explicitly protects against political hypocrisy per se, concerns about self-interested politicians and public representatives who might be more vulnerable to manipulation by foreign powers gave shape to pivotal debates among the Founding Fathers, who drew on Enlightenment philosophers to develop a model of government they believed to be self-sustaining, that would benefit all parties, and that would guard against foreign influence. Drawing on principles central to Adam Smith's *Theory of Moral Sentiments*, the Founders approached the framing of the Constitution as an attempt to protect individual liberty while ensuring that ordinary citizens and elected officials alike acted in the interest of the public good. By using the Constitution to sustain and incentivize good citizenship, its architects established as rule of law the reciprocal agreement implied by the social contract: that with rights come responsibilities.

But though the Founding Fathers sought to design a modern capitalist state that established public trust in the government by establishing ethical boundaries for those in office, they were hamstrung by their concerns about diminishing the electoral power of the people. According to recent scholarship, the architects of the early republic recognized the vulnerability of the union to bad faith actors and were particularly concerned about how men of questionable character might both take advantage of the powers of public office and be taken advantage of by foreign powers. In *Bad for Democracy: How the Presidency Undermines the Power of the People*, Dana Nelson shows how the presidency has developed beyond the limits set for it by the Founding Fathers.[8] Exploring the debates that gave shape to the Constitutional Convention of 1787, Nelson shows how the steadily expanding powers granted to the president (as privileges of the executive branch) have contributed to the erosion of checks and balances designed to hold presidents to a behavioral standard. First published before the 2008 presidential election, Nelson's book is a prescient reminder that the executive office is more vulnerable than ever to a president without principles. If we are surprised by Trump's seemingly inexhaustible ability to shirk his moral responsibilities to the union while pathologically lying to the American public without consequence, we shouldn't be: Republicans have spent decades preparing the political landscape to accommodate and protect a president who will say and do anything for personal gain.

By the time of Trump's election, bad faith arguments were already deeply ingrained at every level of conservative political life in the

United States. The president has merely drawn attention to the latent but pervasive hypocrisy of the modern Republican Party. Perhaps most notable in this regard is the "pro-life" movement, which galvanized the religious right and gave shape to four decades of persistently fraught debates about abortion rights. The term "pro-life" misleadingly implies a politics that is manifestly *anti-death*: proponents of the movement champion the principle that all human life is sacred yet support policies that frame certain lives—of those most different from theirs—as disposable. But whether conservatives voting against abortion rights can be called bad faith actors depends, according to Sartre, on whether they are aware of the contradictions between their stated principles and their actual politics. As Texas state legislators explore a provision that would define abortion as homicide and make it punishable by the death penalty, the extent of this conservative political hypocrisy in regard to human life has become distressingly clear—at least to observers on the left. We can observe evidence of their conservative political passivity toward human life—a relinquishment of responsibility that is characteristic of bad faith—in their refusal to fight for human life in any other political arena. For example, in the debate over gun control, conservatives have for generations adopted a passive stance, shrugging off their moral responsibility to help curb terrorist attacks by white nationalists, offering instead their "thoughts and prayers" to victims—and actively sabotaging attempts by Democrats to bring gun-control legislation before Congress. By throwing up their hands and absolving themselves of responsibility for making it easier for Americans to commit mass murder—and, worse, by tacitly dismissing these deaths as consistent with a divine plan over which they have no control—modern Republicans not only operate in bad faith but also promote and disseminate a "bad faith" interpretation of their own Christian faith.

To argue that pro-life proponents act in bad faith is to assume that they are unaware of their political hypocrisy, or that they operate in a state of denial—that they have convinced themselves of the reliability of their arguments using questionable logic, but have convinced themselves nonetheless. On this particular issue, which has driven a wedge between the two major political parties for generations, and which has become increasingly fraught as evangelical Christians continue to gain control over the Republican agenda, it is difficult to determine the extent to which conservatives are aware of their double standard toward human life. But other, recent examples of political hypocrisy are more clearly indicative of what Sartre would call "cynicism." In these cases, it is hard to believe that the double standard is not entered into knowingly, which raises questions about how we interpret Republican policy in general.

The manufactured hysteria among Republicans over Hillary Clinton's private email server during the 2016 presidential election, for example, can no longer be regarded as having been a serious security concern at the time. Yet the consequences of the cynicism perpetuated by conservative pundits—their inflated sense of propriety where it concerned a political opponent, in contrast to their indifference to their own nominee's flagrant disregard for ethical regulations—were far-reaching. It may be safe to speculate that James Comey's decision to reopen the investigation into Clinton's private email server "probably" cost her the election—yet Comey's letter to Congress on 28 October merely sanctioned a narrative of suspicion engineered by right-wing conspiracy theorists. By this point, the word "emails" had become a trigger word among conservatives. According to a Gallup poll taken between 17 July and 18 September 2016, when asked what they recalled reading, hearing, or seeing about Hillary Clinton in the last day or two, the word "emails" was mentioned three times more frequently than any other word, and was closely followed by the word "lie."

Since the election of Trump, Republicans seem markedly less concerned about cybersecurity in the Oval Office or the Situation Room. They are willing to turn a blind eye to White House security clearance ethics, to the president's unmonitored and unregulated use of social media, and to the Russian cyberattacks that continue to threaten the future of safe and fair democratic elections. If the complaints over Clinton's use of emails in her role as secretary of state were made in good faith and according to an actual moral standard for presidential behavior, Trump would have faced months of Congressional hearings for his decision to discuss North Korean ballistic-missile capabilities in plain view of his Mar-a-Lago guests in 2017. But Republican commentators and Congressional leaders have remained largely silent on the subject of the president's indiscretions precisely because it is not politically expedient for them to consider this legitimate threat to national security. In hindsight, then, the conservative uproar about Clinton's emails had exactly the desired effect: it prompted voters to question her political integrity and to distract from the more serious ethical violations and personal scandals of their own candidate.

By acting with integrity and refusing to mirror the incendiary hyperbole of her opponent, Clinton effectively ceded the presidency to a man who manifestly lacks such integrity. But by doing so, she may have saved the reputation of her own party while exposing the hypocrisies and jeopardizing the future of the other. In view of the Republican Party's bolder, less easily excused violations of public trust that have come to light since the election, it is all the more important that Democratic representatives hold Republicans in Congress accountable for the corruption of ethical standards wrought by their president. This means actively drawing attention to the hypocrisies that cannot be dismissed with recourse to religious belief or personal values, and reinstating a system of checks and balances on presidential ethics.

There is a dire need for those running for and holding elected office to make clear their own positions on policy and to abide by those positions. If they neglect to do the former, then voters' *ability* to choose the person to implement their will is blocked. If they neglect the latter, then the *effect* of voters trying to implement their will is blocked. In either case, hiding or abrogating one's policy positions must be understood as an ethical breach of the most basic aspect of democratic republican government. Voters choose candidates because of justified beliefs that those candidates reflect *their* will and *their* policy preferences. When those in office neglect their previously endorsed positions, they undermine the founding principles of a democratic republic. The time has come to stop accepting hypocrisy in Washington, state capitals, and local government. Politicians must be bound by the arguments, claims, and beliefs they endorse for consumption by the voters. If we lived in a direct democracy, this duplicity might not matter nearly as much. If the people could simply vote their policy preferences, it wouldn't matter what political leaders actually believed. But we don't. We live in a republic. When our leaders loudly endorse a policy preference today, simply to abandon it tomorrow, then citizens are deprived of the opportunity to vote for the candidates who reflect their views. This is not a healthy state for a state to be in.

Women's March in New York City, 20 January 2018.

The current American political system has ruptured this pillar of democracy. Voters can no longer be confident in their beliefs about candidates' positions on many crucial issues. As the old joke suggests, politicians have always been viewed as being less than entirely honest. Still, the republic has held despite a certain amount of dissembling. What distinguishes the politics of today is that even the presumption of truth and consistency has been completely abandoned. When we are careless with our words or when we mischaracterize the positions of our opponents, we are doing a disservice to ourselves and to those who stand beside us. We don't necessarily need to find a middle ground, for there is scarce middle ground to be found these days— but we might find ways to engage on the issues in ways that cannot be weaponized against us.

Notes

1   Jena McGregor, "The Most Memorable Passage in George W. Bush's Speech Rebuking Trumpism," *Washington Post*, 20 October 2017.

2   David French, "America's Worst Congressman Endorses Donald Trump," *National Review*, 1 March 2016.

3   Juliet Eilperin, "Biden and Obama Rewrite the Rulebook on College Sexual Assaults," *Washington Post*, 3 July 2016.

4   Ben Feuerherd, "Two More Women Come Forward with Joe Biden Accusations," *New York Post*, 2 April 2019.

5   John Herrman, "American Politics Is Swamped with 'Bad Faith' Actors," *New York Times Magazine*, 2 January 2018.

6   Megan Garber, "Ye of 'Bad Faith,'" *The Atlantic*, 5 December 2017.

7   David Detmer, *Sartre Explained: From Bad Faith to Authenticity* (Chicago: Carus, 2008), 86.

8   Dana Nelson, *Bad for Democracy: How the Presidency Undermines the Power of the People* (Minneapolis: University of Minnesota Press, 2008).

Chapter One

TRUMP

The Inheritor of the GOP's Southern Strategy

MANY HAVE POINTED TO THE RISE OF THE CONSPIRACY-fringe right in the wake of Obama's election as a possible reason for Trump's victory in 2016, and this is, to say the last, a persuasive argument when considering the similarities between the Tea Party and Make America Great Again (MAGA) movements. However, while the Tea Party and its cadre of resentful, revanchist, white ("working class") voters seemed to suggest the emergence of a new political force—a new vanguard of Republican voters mobilized by a combination of the commander-in-chief's clearly unacceptable levels of melanin and egged on by a chorus of spittle-flecked pundits on America's air and radio waves—something more sinister came into play in the 2016 election. Rush Limbaugh, Sean Hannity, Alex Jones, and Glenn Beck[1] certainly did their part in stoking the fires of white outrage and anti-liberal sentiment that fueled the creation of the Tea Party, but this can't entirely account for the ascendancy and election of Donald Trump.

Make America Great Again hat in support of Donald Trump at a rally at Veterans Memorial Coliseum at the Arizona State Fairgrounds in Phoenix, Arizona, 18 June 2016.

Donald Trump's support, first as a candidate and then as the titular leader of the GOP, is not entirely the outcropping of the nearly ubiquitous rise in nationalist politicians in once-liberal once-democracies around the world,[2] nor is it the result of the DNC's deafness to the real concerns of American voters—this latter critique may justifiably be laid at the feet of establishment democrats, but the Democrats' shortcomings (particularly the considerable shortcomings of its 2016 candidate) did not give us Trump. If we want to understand how we got here, we need to look back further. The seed that gave us this dithering man-baby in the Oval Office was planted much earlier—more than 50 years ago. Trump is the fruition of the GOP's Southern Strategy.

The Southern Strategy—born in the 1950s and coming into force over the following two decades[3]—was an eyes-swollen-shut haymaker swung in the tenth round. At the dawn of the 1960s, Republicans were on the outside looking in. Eisenhower had made the 1950s Republican years, but Democratic presidents had overseen the lion's share of the previous two decades. Kennedy was enjoying approval ratings north of 70 per cent, and Republicans were looking down the barrel at another two terms shut out of the White House—perhaps more if they didn't do something to pull voters away from the

Democrats. What kind of platform could they run on that would erode some of the support in Democratic strongholds (particularly in the South)? Answer: a race-based one.

Republicans began switching into the Democrats' lanes in the late 1950s and early 1960s when they started courting Southern voters, particularly those who were overtly nostalgic for the clear racial hierarchies of the antebellum South. Democrats had long held these voters in the palm of their hands, but they'd begun loosening their grip, heeding some of the calls (albeit slowly) for more egalitarian reforms. Policies grounded in the belief that all men, even Southern negroes, were created equal were anathema to the writers at the recently launched and staunchly conservative *National Review*. Revolution could be scented in the air. The established racial order was under attack, and the writers at the *Review* took up the standard of whites who were deeply interested in preserving that order. They explicitly compared the looming black uprising to the rising threat of communism in Europe and on America's campuses. Racial integration, preached by black radicals and campus communists, was therefore to be resisted by every patriotic American.

On 1 February 1960, four black college students had the audacity to demand service at a Woolworth's lunch counter in Greensboro, North Carolina, refusing to leave until they had been served. They weren't served that day, but after an effective boycott of segregated lunch counters, the owners finally caved and allowed the young black men to rub elbows with their white clientele. At virtually the same time, Barry Goldwater's *The Conscience of a Conservative*, which advocated for states' rights at a time when the federal government was enforcing desegregation, was flying off the shelves in Southern states. Goldwater—a deeply conservative Arizona Republican—lamented the fact that neither party was at that time standing up sufficiently for the right of states to integrate (or not) as they saw fit: "today," he said, "*neither* of our two parties maintains a meaningful commitment to the principle of States' Rights."[4] Goldwater was calling for a new kind of Republican Party—one that put states' rights ahead of civil rights, which he claimed were not sufficiently defined to be legally meaningful.

Goldwater's ideas were, perhaps unsurprisingly, extremely popular in the states that were then integrating at the barrel of a gun. Southern white voters accepted integration either reluctantly or not at all, and there was widespread grumbling about the trampled-upon rights of decent white folk. This made the Southern states ripe for the picking; they believed themselves to be the aggrieved parties—every inch of the black man's progress was, in effect, an encroachment on *their* rights, on *white rights*. Democrats had not done enough to keep the black man in his place in the South, and with each passing year they were doing less. That blacks could vote was bad enough, but now they wanted to eat at the same lunch counter and go to the same schools as whites? This couldn't be allowed to stand.

The founder of the *National Review*, William F. Buckley—who had already spoken in print about the "advanced" white race and about the need for the South to "prevail" in the face of calls for integration—took up the banner of Southern whites, putting in black and white what so many of them were thinking. Compared to the whites of the deep South, the negroes, he said, were "retarded."[5] This wasn't a dog whistle so much as it was a bullhorn for racist Southerners fed up with America's drift toward racial toleration.

Over the next few years, the *Review* frequently took the side of Southern whites in their ongoing struggle to resist integration, and in February 1963, the periodical's publisher William Rusher outlined in broad strokes the Southern Strategy in the pages of the *Review*. He said that Barry Goldwater had the best chance of winning, and winning in a way that Republicans had not yet tried. By moving the party platform significantly to the right (which Goldwater would undoubtedly do), the Republicans could effectively beat the Democrats at their own game in the South. They could take the South out of Democratic hands and, with it, perhaps the presidency as well.

Of course, Goldwater's campaign, based on its results on election night, was an utter disaster. Thanks in large part to Goldwater's terrifyingly hawkish stance (critiqued heavy-handedly in LBJ's infamous "Daisy" TV ad, which seemed to threaten complete annihilation of the United States in the event of an LBJ loss), Johnson ran away with the race, winning 61 per cent of the popular vote (the largest share since the uncontested 1820 election). Still, even though he was an unsuccessful presidential candidate, Goldwater's Southern Strategy completely upended the electoral map. The formerly deep-blue states of Alabama, Louisiana, Mississippi, Georgia, and South Carolina all turned red, and white Southerners felt like they had a party that spoke *directly* to their anxieties about race. LBJ's Democrats no longer spoke on behalf of aggrieved Southern whites, and Johnson made this clear when he signed the *Civil Rights Act* of 1964 only months before the general election, knowing that this would cost him the South for a generation. Goldwater donned the mantle of the Great White Hope, making the Republican platform one of opposition (opposition, he said, on constitutional grounds) to the *Civil Rights Act*. What's more, he had given cover to right-wing extremist groups like the Ku Klux Klan and the John Birch Society, saying during the campaign that (white) extremism was "no vice" when it was in support of "liberty."[6]

This dramatic rightward movement (and its success in the South) was the defining moment that formed the outline of what the modern Republican Party would become. When Trump (whom nobody would call a student of history) says that the Republican Party can't *possibly* be racist because Abraham Lincoln was a Republican, he is assuming (usually correctly) that his audience is either unaware or willfully ignorant of the GOP's history—especially its decision (made in plain view) to openly court the white-supremacist vote. This is how, 50 years after the *National Review* proposed Goldwater as a candidate, the party that once advocated for Southern slaveholders is now the party with presidential candidates seriously discussing reparations; it's how the party of Lincoln became the party of "very fine people on both sides."[7]

Goldwater's campaign showed Republicans that it was possible to win in the South without *any* numerically significant support from black voters. Goldwater received only six per cent of the Black vote, as opposed to Eisenhower's 39 per cent in 1956 and Nixon's 32 per cent in 1960.[8] Though there may have been hand-wringing about the growing numerical superiority of blacks in some Southern communities, black voters weren't able to tip the scales. Black communities utterly repudiated Goldwater, but that rejection simply wasn't enough when Southern whites were presented with a candidate who knew the Song of the South by heart. White voters prevailed at the polling places, turning the South a deep and lasting red. The Republican had whistled Dixie, and Dixie had come running.

By the next election cycle, Nixon, who had formerly presented himself as a civil rights champion when courting Northern black voters in his 1960 campaign, was openly embracing the Southern Strategy, pairing it with deeply conservative policies like opposition to social welfare and claiming to speak for the "silent majority" and the "forgotten American." He referred to himself as the "law and order" candidate—coded language that suggested he would take a very different tack with the black rioters who had made the summer of 1967 so very long and so very hot for urban whites. The Republican Party gave itself over entirely to this wooing of white voters while simultaneously cloaking itself in evangelical sanctimoniousness. As hypocritical as this combination was, it was a winning formula for Republicans. Thanks in no small part to the north-moving wave of racial anxiety, Nixon and the GOP rode on the backs of white voters (particularly evangelical ones) to Pennsylvania Avenue, taking the White House and, with the exception of Carter's single term, holding it until, in 1992, the Democrats ran their own Southern boy: Bill Clinton.

With Goldwater's campaign, the GOP rolled over and exposed its white-supremacist underbelly. Lily-white Republicans and other white-supremacist factions of the GOP had long been working to disenfranchise Southern blacks and appease Southern whites,[9] but the party had still managed to paint itself as the natural home for black voters. Goldwater changed all this by saying publicly what many white Republicans espoused privately. This allowed the GOP to corner the market on white-supremacist voters.

The GOP was not a uniformly white-supremacist party when it adopted the Southern Strategy in the 1960s, but the Goldwater campaign was a watershed moment. In the decades that followed, an undercurrent of troubling racial ideologies and problematic allegiances percolated only inches below the surface of the party's official platform. It has never made anything more than a back-handed attempt to exorcize its racist demons, choosing instead to continue its pandering to Southern whites with racially coded nostalgia. Its longed-for halcyon age has, since the 1960s, been the simpler time when GIs returned from overseas and started a family in a suburban home with a white picket fence, a bubbling pot, and an American car in the driveway. This was (and still is) the America of nostalgic whites—America before her troubles (i.e., her movement toward some semblance of equality) began.

Racism was (and still is) coded into Republican nostalgia. It bubbled beneath the surface of the party, which primed the GOP for a candidate like Donald Trump to bring the party's *id* to the surface—a candidate, and then a president, who would work actively to create what William Barber calls "immoral acts of deconstruction"[10] (those nostalgic and regressive policies that push back decades of progress). While talking heads dismissed Trump as a radical fringe candidate, the candidate was shoring up support with his blatantly xenophobic and Islamophobic rhetoric. The fact that he had racially discriminated against black tenants as a real-estate developer and that he had called for the return of the death penalty with a full-page ad when the Central Park Five had been falsely accused didn't disqualify him in the minds of deeply conservative voters—if anything, his history of racism made him a *more* viable candidate. The GOP had been courting these voters, putting forth candidates who were clever enough to use coded racist language. The white supremacist vote has been theirs for generations, but now they had something they hadn't expected—a candidate who wore his white supremacy on his lapel.

While some establishment Republicans joined the chorus of Democrats who objected to Trump's candidacy on moral or political grounds, the rank and file quickly fell into line behind him the moment it became clear that the nomination was his to lose. Sure he was incompetent, sure he was unable to clearly articulate policy (or, for that matter, opinion), sure he was a liar who would say almost anything to anybody, but Trump had won the rabid support of the GOP's until-then-unacknowledged base: white males (and a surprising number of white females as well—surprising considering the candidate's proclivities) who were keen to turn back the clock to when America was "great" (i.e., racially pure and nominally Christian).

The Southern Strategy had started as an out-and-out rejection of black advancement, but in its later incarnations it came to lean on coded language and dog whistles: Nixon's "law and order," Reagan's "young buck," and Bush Sr.'s Willie Horton ad, just to name a few. There were *implications* that minorities were, at best, burdens on the state and, at worst, prone to criminality, but the audience was expected to connect the dots, which gave the speaker cover in the form of plausible deniability. This cover was ripped away on the day that Trump descended the Trump Tower escalator to officially announce his candidacy. He revived the Southern Strategy by speaking *directly and unashamedly* to white-supremacist voters, making explicit what had, for decades, been hidden beneath layers of coded language. He was inviting white nationalists, white supremacists, and your garden-variety bigots to crawl out from beneath their rocks—and crawl out they did. They had their champion.

As Trump rose through the Republican ranks during the primaries, he parroted talk radio pundits and elevated conspiracy theorists formerly relegated to internet backwaters. Like Goldwater, he went out of his way to appeal to America's deepest and oldest prejudices and fears. His campaign was not aspirational—it was revanchist. The progress of the last century had come at the expense of the white man's security in his house on the hill. For Goldwater, the savages were banging at the gates; for Trump, they have broken down the walls and the front door and are settling themselves by the fire. In his vision of America, it is no longer a matter of protecting what white America has—it's about getting back what has been taken.

When Trump refused to condemn the red-hatted white supremacists in Charlottesville, it was because their war chants were only one degree removed from what his rally crowds have screamed (often in unison) since day one of his campaign. The red hats who chant at Trump's rallies and the brown shirts who marched in Charlottesville may not be ideologically identical, but they have both rallied behind the same leader. They see themselves as fighting on the same side of the same war: they are foot soldiers in the culture wars, and Trump is their general. He will *never* disavow the support of the army he mobilized—to do so would be the equivalent of cutting his political legs out from beneath him. He knows he can't win in 2020 without their support.

* * *

During his campaign, Trump invoked Nixon's so-called silent majority (the millions of go-along-get-along Americans who, rather than protesting the Vietnam War or otherwise challenging received wisdom about the goodness of country and capital, kept mum and voted conservatively). Nixon's framing of conservative voters in this way was a political masterstroke. It reminded this considerable voting bloc that they were still in control. Even if America was changing around them, they were (and would remain) in the majority. The suggestion was that American policies, with Nixon at the helm, would continue to put the interests of white Americans above all others. Trump (or, more likely, his handlers) dusted off this idea and brought it back into use (part of a general pattern of jingo recycling from Republican campaigns of the not-so-distant past). Crowds cheerfully waved placards at rallies that proclaimed, "the silent majority stands with Trump," but now the context had changed. Nixon's silent majority was concerned with protecting what they felt was, by right, their own; Trump's silent majority saw things differently. They were not silent protectors of the status quo. Quite the opposite, they needed protecting from the status quo. The moral needle had moved substantially between Nixon's campaign and Trump's. Trump's base was not so much the silent majority as it was a minority that felt it had been silenced and sidelined by redefined American values and broadly accepted notions of political correctness.

Republican presidents before Trump surely understood that the nation's moral needle had shifted considerably. When, for instance, David Duke ran in Louisiana for a seat in the US Senate in 1991, George H.W. Bush would have none of it. He addressed Louisianans, telling them that the former Klansman was not fit for a leadership role.[11] Duke still managed to pick up an astonishing 60 per cent of the white vote in Louisiana, but this wasn't enough to propel him to victory (only the mobilization of black voters kept him from being seated in the Senate). Duke's base was described in virtually the same terms as Trump's: "working class" whites who, according to Susan Howell, then-director of the Survey Research Center at the University of New Orleans, had a "tremendous amount of anger and frustration" (apparently the result of an economic downturn).[12] Then, as now, pollsters were keen to show that those who voted for openly white-supremacist candidates were not themselves white supremacists. Rather, they were sending Washington a message (that message came in the form of the worst Son of the South they could mark an X beside).

When, eight years later, H.W.'s son, George W. Bush, was running for the presidency, he too did his part to place distance between white supremacists and the GOP (but not *too* much distance). He disavowed David Duke, who had thrown his and his supporters' considerable weight behind the candidacy of Pat Buchanan, but he punted when asked during a 2000 televised debate what he thought about the Confederate Flag that flew over the South Carolina State House, saying that "the people of South Carolina can figure out what to do with this flag issue"[13] (this elicited raucous applause from the home crowd and a smirk from Bush—obviously pleased with himself). Unlike Trump, though, Bush didn't wax poetically about America's precious history and culture; he didn't assign himself as the defender of the monuments to men (glorious in Southern memory) who fought on the losing side to preserve the South's right to keep black bodies in chains.

Bush, drawl and all, cultivated an image of himself as a good ol' boy, but this had its limits. He disavowed, on numerous occasions, Buchanan's and Duke's "politics of hate," he said that "Islam is peace" in the wake of 9/11 when anti-Muslim sentiment was rising sharply, and, when his presidency was over, he told an interviewer that the moment when Kanye West announced on live television that Bush didn't care about black people was the worst moment of his presidency. This is by no means a defense of Bush or the GOP during the Bush years. The GOP's policies in the early part of this century were still targeting blacks and other minorities unfairly, still imprisoning black bodies at alarming rates, and yes, the government's laggardly response to Hurricane Katrina revealed a great deal about how the party and its president viewed black communities (especially in the South). The party did, however, clearly care about how it was perceived by minority communities. It may have still *been* a racist party, but it didn't *feel* racist.

What a difference eight years made. The resistance to Obama in conservative media and at protests and rallies leaned heavily on racist tropes and caricatures, becoming bolder as the Tea Party grew, transforming from a fiscally conservative political movement into a catch-all for anti-liberal outrage junkies and race-baiters. Trump leaned into this hard, throwing all of his 239 pounds into the racist birther movement, becoming the unofficial leader of the movement. In the person of Trump, white supremacists found a popular figure who shared their views on the president and his illegitimacy. He spouted the same conspiracy theories and moved to the front and center some formerly fringe elements of the party. There was never any doubt that, when Trump announced his candidacy, he already had the white-supremacist vote deep in his pocket.

Trump's revived Southern Strategy was inconsistent at first. When his campaign was less than two weeks old, he told a reporter that South Carolina should take down the Confederate flag and put it in a museum (something that surely drew the ire of the Southern whites who might have been listening), but, as his crowds grew, so too did the clearly white-supremacist contingent, and Trump began drifting further and further into the kind of territory they wanted to see him explore. By the beginning of 2016, he was retweeting white supremacists—one with the handle @WhiteGenocideTM—and white-supremacist groups were using Trump's campaign as a rallying point. *Stormfront*, the most popular online white-supremacist portal, had to upgrade its servers to cope with the increased traffic that Trump's campaign was bringing to its site; the site's founder said, "Demoralization has been the biggest enemy and Trump is changing all that."[14] Hate groups felt energized and emboldened, and, to approximately nobody's surprise, hate crimes have been on the rise since Trump's campaign began.[15] His responses each time there is a Muslim terror attack in Europe, his Muslim ban, his hardline immigration policies that have created thousands of brown-skinned orphans—these are all straight out of the white-supremacist playbook.

While it is a mischaracterization to say that all Trump supporters are racists, it is undeniably true that, under the MAGA tent, you'll find far more intolerant Americans than you'll find outside of it. You might very well find a fringe element under the Democratic tent, but you'd be hard pressed to find a Democratic voter who thinks a white ethno-state is the solution to what ails America. Under the Republican tent, though, you can't cast a stone in any direction without striking a bigot. Intolerance is part and parcel of the GOP brand, and the polling numbers bear this out. In a PPP poll prior to the South Carolina primary in 2016, 38 per cent of Trump supporters said they wished the Confederacy had won the Civil War; 70 per cent of them felt the Confederate flag should be flying over the South Carolina Capitol building, and 16 per cent of them believed that whites are the superior race.[16] Trump didn't create these voters, and the GOP didn't create them either, but the party has started to reflect their white supremacy in alarming ways. Professor Michael Tesler, a researcher at the University of California at Irvine, wrote in the *Washington Post* that "the Republican Party's growing conservatism on matters of race and ethnicity provided fertile ground for Trump's racial and ethnic appeals to resonate in the primaries [...] Donald Trump is the first

Republican in modern times to win the party's presidential nomination on anti-minority sentiments."[17] It's not exactly clear what Tesler
means by "modern times," for Reagan vilified black welfare queens
and gestured toward the menace of young black men on the campaign
trail, but these were, it is true, only the sideshow to the main event.
Trump brought racial anxieties to the very center of his platform.

Trump's racial scapegoating found purchase not only in the
deeply racist South but also in the rust belt, which, in places, is
every bit as racist as the deep South. Middle schoolers in Royal Oak,
Michigan, broke out into chants of "Build the wall" in class only days
after Trump's victory; in the same state, only a few days later, an off-
duty police officer was suspended for waving a Confederate flag as
he argued with anti-Trump protesters.[18] Are these outliers? Are they
representative of Trump's base, or can they be dismissed with a wave
of the hand as a few bad apples?

Pundits seem determined to prove the bad apple hypothesis.
They have twisted themselves into knots attempting to prove that
it was economic and not racial anxieties that helped propel Trump
to sweeping victories in formerly blue states. These are the "working class" voters that were promised a return to the good old days
of good-paying factory jobs. While these voters do exist, and while
they may, indeed, have tipped the scales in Wisconsin, Michigan,
and Pennsylvania, they weren't responsible for Trump's name being
on the ballot in the first place. That dubious distinction goes to the
white-supremacist voters—those same voters the GOP has been
openly courting since Goldwater.

It looked, for a time, as though the Republican Party would abandon these voters. In the wake of the GOP's defeat in the 2012 election,
there was a sudden interest in reaching minority voters. If the GOP
was to survive, it needed to start reflecting in its membership and its
policies the changing face of the country. The Republican Party was,
once again, staring into the abyss—looking into a future in which it
would be increasingly sidelined. Trump's birtherism and rumblings
about being the kind of man who could fix what was wrong with
America were covered widely by the media, but few people imagined
that the sideshow would goosestep its way into the center ring. It did
this, not by modernizing the party, but by leaning into the criticisms
leveled at it. For a brief moment, the GOP tried to rebrand itself as

a party for all, but most saw this as a cynical, bad-faith move—for that's exactly what it was. Trump, as he tore through the primary field, made it clear that the GOP was not going to look forward if he had anything to say about it. It was going to be a backward-facing party. It was going to be the *only* party (and he the *only* candidate) that would encourage whites to be proud of their culture.

What is that culture they're so proud of? What is it exactly that they're so keen to restore and defend? Is it monster-truck shows and shooting ranges? Mega-churches and the Appalachian Trail? Axe body spray and the Confederate flag? When pressed, the culture warriors will speak broadly about European or Western culture or perhaps about Judeo-Christian values, but the groups that coalesced around Trump, first as a candidate and then as president, aren't making pilgrimages to Europe. They don't connect to Europe's culture—they connect to the skin color of Europeans. They connect to distinctly European strains of nationalism and to their deep-seated orientalism—not to the works of the mind and spirit that shaped Europe and her peoples.

No, culture has nothing to do with it. At least in the minds of Trump devotees, European or Western culture boils down to *white* culture and, with just a few more moments over the fire, to whiteness itself. Speaking about Western culture and European heritage is a barely-there cover for white supremacy.[19] Trump is no cultural warrior—he's a race warrior, and he's mobilized an army of trolls and race-baiters who are tired of speaking one way when shielded by closed doors or anonymous forums and another way in public. They wanted a candidate who would say out loud what they were thinking, and they found one in Trump.

Trump has been framed (indeed, has framed himself) as the antidote to political correctness—as a straight shooter with little to no concern for how his words are perceived. Liberal America keeps waiting for the other shoe to drop, for his latest outrage to produce plummeting approval numbers, but this ignores the fact that his base (Southern whites and their ideological ilk) doesn't see the outrages that seem to fall out of Trump's mouth almost daily as remotely problematic. They cheer more loudly when he is blatantly racist and excuse him his "locker-room talk." His base has asked Trump for Liberal tears, and he has responded with a seemingly endless barrage of policies and executive orders that seem to have no purpose other than to dismantle what remains of Obama's progressive legacy. The outrage sparked by his rending of environmental and consumer protections and democratic norms is not falling on deaf ears—it's music to their ears. Each time Trump ignores a subpoena or plays lickspittle to a tin-pot dictator, the left howls in protest and Trump's base cheers—first comes the howl of outrage from the left, and then the cheer from Trump's base. The order is important: they are not cheering the action itself, only its response from Democrats and progressives.

Trump ran to be the troll-in-chief, and his supporters are loving every minute of it. There's nothing he can do—no inanity or goal-line fumble too great—that would cause his support to dry up. He speaks almost exclusively to and for his base—the 35 to 40 per cent of the country who would walk single file into the Atlantic if Trump asked them to. In their eyes, Trump is America's Great White Hope, and his ascendance to and continued presence in the Oval Office shows (and I'd agree, it *does* show) that white resentment is coming off the sidelines and becoming politically active in ways we haven't seen since Reagan's presidency.

It may be tempting to see Trump as something new, as an aberration produced by a particular (and short-lived) moment in time, but he is actually something very old. He was a candidate and is now a president who is craven enough to embrace the core of the Southern Strategy (i.e., the undisputable fact that an overtly racist campaign, thanks to the support of white supremacist voters, particularly in the South, can carry a politician all the way to the White House). The depressing reality is that white supremacists and those who tolerate them make up a considerable voting bloc: according to recent polling, 10 per cent of the country finds it perfectly acceptable to hold white-supremacist views; only 72 per cent of Americans feel strongly that white-supremacist views are unacceptable.[20] Trump needs this 28 per cent of Americans. Far from disavowing his white-supremacist support, Trump makes it clear each day that he depends on it—just as they depend on him, and this dependence has, says Amy Siskind, "pulled America into a new age of chaos and white supremacy."[21] It has rewritten the rules for what is acceptable in Washington, and it may be some time before we have returned to at least a semblance of political normalcy.

There were undeniably many reasons that Trump's supporters voted for him, and they may vote for him again in 2020 for the same reasons (none of them based on race). Economic concerns remain at the top of the heap for many voters, and Trump has thus far managed to avoid the kind of recession that would send his wallet-minding voters scurrying. Others may have been convinced (and may still be convinced) by the scare-mongering surrounding progressive politics and what has been presented by right-wing commentators as the steady erosion of personal freedoms that Democrats will bring in their wake. Others might be single-issue voters, who stand with Trump solely because of his promise to stack the courts with conservative judges who will overturn *Roe v. Wade* or protect Americans' right to bear arms. Still others, convinced that Trump is the anti-politician *par excellence*, might be taken in by the cult of personality and difference surrounding the president. None of these voters are necessarily white supremacists, and painting all of Trump's supporters with such a wide brush is certainly not my intention here. Still, those who have found themselves beneath the Republican tent in the last election, thanks to their support for Trump, are to at least some degree complicit in what has followed. They've made their bed, and now they must lie in it, sharing it with the white supremacists and the misogynists, and all the other deplorable bedbugs that helped propel Trump to victory and continue to prop up his squalid administration. For those who pulled the lever for Trump who pay even the slightest bit of attention to what is happening in their country, and who care about human dignity and America's standing in the world (about *actual* not imaginary American greatness), this must be a difficult time. Squaring their vote with their conscience surely can't be easy.

For those who didn't vote for Trump in 2016, or for those who have come to regret their vote for him, the problem is different. What do we do about a problem like Trump? More particularly, what can we do about his newly emboldened white-supremacist followers and others who don full-throated support for this man? On December 18th, 2019, Nancy Pelosi's House of Representatives pulled the trigger on impeachment of Donald Trump in a 230–197 vote. What the Democrats called an effort to restore good faith in the function of the checks-and-balances system, the Republicans called a hastily constructed scam. Nevertheless, for only the third time in American history, a sitting President was impeached. Donald Trump's removal of office, however, requires a seventy-five percent approval from the 100 U.S. Senators, a feat that Senate Minority Leader Mitch McConnell vows will never happen. What will come of this political theater is unknown, but we—progressives, people of color, and all those in this country with a moral conscience—can do and must do something about the red-hat army of morally constipated sycophants that Trump has mobilized.

To begin with, we need to do everything we can to mobilize an army of our own, and this means that we on the left must cohere and galvanize. We must revive an insistent and irrepressible hope—a familiar but all-but-forgotten hope in these despairing times. During the Obama years, change (and change for the better) scented the air. On a cool November evening in 2008, standing on a stage in Chicago's Grant Park, Obama looked over a multi-colored patchwork of supporters. With tears in their eyes, the crowd chanted slogans of hope and change: "Yes we can," they said—and they believed it. The high expectations were palpable then, and they remained so throughout Obama's presidency—even in the face of business as usual in Washington and a string of disappointments for progressives.

Obama couldn't close—at least not in any significant way—the gap between black and white unemployment. His EPA responded far too slowly and ineffectually to the drinking water crisis in Flint, Michigan, worsening the problem. Though he promised to deport "felons not families," only around 40 per cent of the people he deported during his presidency had criminal records; deportations actually rose under his watch, earning him the moniker Deporter in Chief from immigrant advocacy groups.[22] The response to the Standing Rock protestors was brutally heavy-handed—even if there was little that Obama could have done to intervene without setting a dangerous precedent in terms of overreach. Racist policing (and the continued reluctance to punish officers who took the lives of unarmed black civilians) continued largely unabated, even if there was increased coverage thanks to Black Lives Matter forcing the issue into the national spotlight.

Though Obama was not the progressive savior many hoped he would be, there was a sense in our communities that we had an ally in the White House. Our concerns were truly being heard—even if the Obama White House's responses to these concerns were being balanced with centrist or right-of-center policy priorities. Congress was unwilling to compromise in any way with Obama, and it was therefore unrealistic to expect him to ram through a progressive agenda. Obama got less than he wanted from Congress, and we got less than we wanted from him. As satisfying as it might have been to see Obama make much more extensive use of executive power, the right would have made hay with this kind of executive overreach. They would have had more success painting him as a tyrant, and it would have set the table for a bad-faith successor like Trump to do even more with his authority than he has done. Based on Obama's emotional responses to progressive causes, he surely would have done more on gun control, health care, and criminal justice reform if he had had good-faith allies on both sides of the aisle, but that simply wasn't the case.

As Obama's second term wound to its close, progressive hopes began to fizzle as they looked at the future. Hillary Clinton's steady march to the DNC nomination left wanting those who wanted a candidate *more* progressive than Obama. Her unclear message failed to resonate deeply with voters, and she treated key swing states as though they were flyovers. Enthusiasm sagged, and on election night, hope—already straining at the seams—was rent entirely. Since then, with outrage piled upon outrage, Trump has battered bloody what little hope remained. The culture wars have quite suddenly become battles on multiple fronts, and on each of these fronts (race relations, reproductive rights, the environment, and LGBTQ causes, to name just a few), progressive forces seem to be losing ground.

It's only natural to feel overwhelmed by it all. With one criminal probe, one outrage, one hopeless case of ineptitude and top-down rot after another, it becomes more and more difficult to muster any of the courage and conviction needed to continue fighting the good fight. That the administration is corrupt, incompetent, and misinformed is bad enough, but the deeper problem is the red-hatted white supremacists who have been waiting for, even praying for, a president exactly like Donald Trump. These emboldened and ascendant white supremacists should not sap our hope for the future of this nation, though; if anything, they should be a clarion call—a reinvigoration of our purpose. It falls on us to show them that Trump's presidency is an aberration—a momentary backward slide. We need (as progressive voices have always needed) to poke and prod America to do the right thing, to push hard against the iron rod of tradition, bending it, slowly but surely, toward equality and justice.

We need to rebuild trust in our institutions, in the good faith or our leadership at both national and local levels, and—at the most basic level—in the ability of democratic engagement to produce long-awaited and long-overdue outcomes. For some of us, that trust has never truly existed. We had only begun to believe in the good faith of our leadership when the ground fell out from beneath our feet. In 2008, we felt, for just a moment as we stood expectantly in the crisp evening air in Chicago's Grant Park, as though the country had turned a corner, but our hopes were quickly disappointed. Obama's presidency (and particularly how Southern whites and their ilk responded to a black man in the Oval Office from day one) proved definitely that the hardest part of the journey toward reconciliation is still ahead of us.[23]

For the briefest moment, we thought that we felt the slightest surge of acceleration. We were, at least during Obama's first term, moving toward that reconciliation—albeit glacially. In the South and the rust belt, though, white voters rallied around peddlers of the politics of racial resentment. Emboldened, Republicans in dark red states effectively disenfranchised minority voters with the aid of voter ID laws that suppressed turnout and with gerrymandering that rendered the already-quiet political voices of minorities all but mute. Especially in the deep South, we witnessed a widening of the divide between the parties on racial lines, with not just Trump but also with GOP senators and state representatives openly embracing the Southern Strategy, capitalizing on white America's anxieties about demographic replacement and identity politics.

Trump didn't create the racial anxieties that made white people in America feel as though they were losing, but he did exploit them, embracing the Southern Strategy in a way that no serious presidential candidate has done since Reagan. Trump's successful presidential campaign and his continued presence in the Oval Office are troubling for many reasons, but most of all for his all-too-successful revival of the politics of white resentment. We must make sure that this revival is short-lived. The next demagogue in line (and there will certainly be others who will try to duplicate Trump's formula) may try to exploit the same anxieties that made Trump's campaign success-ful. We must make sure that the Southern Strategy revival does not become a broadly viable strategy. We do this by handing the GOP a string of defeats that force them back to the position they were considering at the beginning of Obama's term—namely, reposition-ing the GOP as a party that is no longer the natural home for white supremacists. We do this by first sending disinterested and honest leaders to Washington and then having them take a long, hard look at the institutions that allowed a manifestly unqualified and a patently unfit man to rise to the office of presidency (I'm looking at you, elec-toral college).

Finally, we do this by policing our political and civil discourse. Political debate in America has never been entirely friendly, but it has been, for the most part, civilized. When Trump threw his hat in the ring, our discourse became barbaric—it started reflecting the worst sides of our nature, and it gave hope to those who would drag this country backward by purifying it of what they feel are the undesir-ables. The moment the GOP gave Trump a pass for insulting a war hero (which he continues to do while the man lies in his grave) and Gold Star parents, a clear message was sent to the worst of us: the gloves are off. All is now permissible.

The toxification of our discourse has clouded our minds, and only unclouded minds can transcend—and we *need* transcendence. Mired in shortsightedness and stupidity, we have entirely lost sight of this country's potential. When Trump's presidency grinds to what may just be a nationally humiliating end, we must transcend the muck and madness and catch sight, once again, of the horizon unclouded. Virginia Woolf, in *A Room of One's Own*, says that the mind must be "incandescent," that our mind must have "consumed all impedi-ments." We, like the troubled female writers of whom Woolf writes, are "harassed and distracted with hates and grievances. The human race is split up [...] into two parties."[24] Thus divided, we cannot pro-duce the works of genius of which we, as a country, are capable. We are not burning brightly. We are troubled—deeply troubled—and worried about both the present and the future. Every work of this age bears the imprint of these troubles, and until these troubles are past us, we will stand on this spot, rooted to the present, unable to lift our species to the next leap that we must take.

This doesn't mean we need to somehow remove white supremacists from the United States. The necessary work can be done (indeed, must be done) without them. The current of racism in this country is far too deep, its pull far too strong to wipe it out in the span of a generation or even a few of them. There may always be a home for racists in the South and, indeed, in the North as well. We do, however, need to push them back to where they belong—to beyond the border of the acceptable, where they can brood and breed in their miserable hovels. They must be exiled entirely before we can, with minds unclouded, get back to the business of building a more perfect union.

Notes

1   During the 2016 election, Beck said that opposing Trump was a "moral, ethical choice," but he still did a great deal of the heavy lifting in creating the conspiracy-clouded climate of white outrage that made Trump's election possible. He's since changed his tune, saying that Trump's loss in 2020 will mean the "end of the country as we know it," pointing to the "radicals, the anarchists, the Islamists, [and] the socialists" who would, he said, work together to "destabilize Europe and America." Clark Mindock, "Glenn Beck Warns Sean Hannity That Trump Loss in 2020 Would Be 'End of US as We Know It,'" *Independent*, 19 March 2019.

2   Particularly in Britain, Australia, Germany, France, Austria, Hungary, Spain, Sweden, Finland, and the Netherlands, where far-right politicians have ridden opposition to immigration (particularly Muslim immigration) and globalism to prominent seats at the big table.

3   This was actually something of a rebirth. The first Southern Strategy took place in the years following the Civil War, centering around Southern Whites and their resistance to newly established blacks during Reconstruction.

4   Barry Goldwater, *The Conscience of a Conservative* (Princeton, NJ: Princeton UP, 1960), 17.

5   Kevin M. Schultz, "William F. Buckley and *National Review*'s Vile Race Stance: Everything You Need to Know about Conservatives and Race," *Salon*, 7 June 2015.

6   Julian Zelizer, "Risk for GOP comes from extreme fringe," *CNN*, 30 March 2010.

7   President Trump made this statement in 2018 when referring to white supremacists who marched in Charlottesville, Virginia, and the protesters who

were against their presence, instead of denouncing the language of the fire-wielding Nazis and white supremacists.

8   Edward Miller, "When Texas Fell to the Wingnuts: The Secret History of the Southern Strategy, Modern Conservatism and the Lone Star State," *Salon*, 2 November 2015.

9   Leah Wright Rigeur, "The Forgotten History of Black Republicans," *Daily Beast*, 12 February 2015.

10 Rev. William J. Barber II, *The Third Reconstruction: Moral Monday, Fusion Politics, and the Rise of a New Justice Movement* (Boston: Beacon Press, 2016), 115.

11 Roberto Suro, "Bush Denounces Duke as Racist and Charlatan," *New York Times*, 7 November 1991.

12 Adam Serwer, "The Nationalist's Delusion," *The Atlantic*, 20 November 2017.

13 Interview aired 17 February 2000; "Bush: 'People of South Carolina Can Solve' Issue of Confederate Flag over State Capitol," http://transcripts.cnn.com/TRANSCRIPTS/0002/17/se.04.html.

14 Ben Schreckinger, "White Supremacist Groups See Trump Bump," *Politico*, 10 December 2015.

15 Ibid.

16 Lynn Vavreck, "Measuring Donald Trump's Supporters for Intolerance," *New York Times*, 23 February 2016.

17 Michael Tesler, "Trump Is the First Modern Republican to Win the Nomination Based on Racial Prejudice," *Washington Post*, 1 August 2016.

18 Tasreen Nashrula, "Here Are 28 Reported Racist and Violent Incidents after Donald Trump's Victory," *BuzzFeed News*, 15 November 2016.

19 Their focus on European culture also allows them to ignore (conveniently) the distinctly American art forms (blues, jazz, and hip-hop, to name a few) that are inextricably intertwined with blackness. Boiled down, European culture is a creamy pink; American culture is a deep indigo.

20 Gary Langer, "1 in 10 Say It's Acceptable to Hold White Supremacist Views (Poll)," *ABC News*, 21 August 2017.

21 Amy Siskind, *The List: A Week-by-Week Reckoning of Trump's First Year* (New York: Bloomsbury, 2018), xi.

22 See my *Racial Realities and Post-Racial Dreams* (Peterborough, ON: Broadview, 2016), 92.

23 Ibid., 23–24.

24 Virginia Woolf, *A Room of One's Own* (London: Hogarth Press, 1929).

Chapter Two

SHIFTING THE GOALPOST

Poli-Tricks and the Art of Political Gerrymandering

IN THE FALL OF 2018, COMMENTATORS SPECULATED excitedly on the possibility that the nation's first-ever black female governor might be elected—in, of all places, Georgia. Stacey Abrams, State House minority leader and voting-rights activist, combined progressive policy ideas like gun-control measures, Medicaid expansion, and the removal of certain Confederate monuments with more moderate Democratic initiatives like drug-treatment policies and infrastructure initiatives that she had worked effectively across the aisle.[1] As minority leader she collaborated with Republican governor Nathan Deal on scholarship packages and public transportation,[2] as well as criminal-justice reforms credited with significant reductions in Georgia's overall prison population and recidivism rate as well as the incarceration rate for black Georgians. As governor, Abrams promised she would build on that legacy, providing more support for prisoner re-entry, reforming the juvenile justice system, and ending capital punishment. Her opponent, Brian Kemp, offered a vision of criminal-justice reform focused on targeting gang members and undocumented immigrants.[3] Both sides made their cases passionately and publicly.

But the contest for voters' hearts and minds ran parallel with a controversy over who should be allowed to vote. Kemp, as Georgia's secretary of state, had oversight of voter registrations, and there had been many years of controversy about how he used that power. During his tenure as secretary, he removed more than 1.4 million people from the voter rolls.[4] Some of the procedures he oversaw for "combating voter fraud" disproportionately affected minority communities—who were growing to be an ever-larger part of the Georgia electorate as black Americans from the Northeast and Midwest moved to Georgia, causing some to expect a possible Democratic resurgence in the state.[5] The perception of racial bias in voter regulations led to several lawsuits before the 2018 election, which we'll revisit later, as well as an ongoing lawsuit filed after the election[6] and an ongoing investigation by the US House Committee on Oversight and Reform.[7] Kemp, in turn, called for investigations into the New Georgia Project, a voter-registration group focused on minorities which Abrams had spearheaded before leaving to campaign for the governorship.[8]

Kemp explained these investigations and his voter-roll purges as attempts to prevent people from gaming the system through voter fraud. Abrams, on the other hand, saw his policies as attempts to rig the system from the top. She said in her concession speech, "I acknowledge that former Secretary of State Brian Kemp will be certified as the victor in the 2018 gubernatorial election.... But to watch an elected official who claims to represent the people in the state baldly pin his hopes for election on the suppression of the people's democratic right to vote has been truly appalling. So, to be clear, this is not a speech of concession. Concession means to acknowledge an action is right, true or proper. As a woman of conscience and faith, I cannot concede. But my assessment is that the law currently allows no further viable remedy."[9]

The question of how closely law and justice track together also came into play in Florida's 2018 midterm election, when black Democratic Tallahassee mayor Andrew Gillum ran for governor on issues including criminal-justice reform, Medicaid expansion, and the removal of Confederate monuments,[10] against white Republican Ron DeSantis. In this campaign, as in the Georgia race, there was an intense struggle not only to appeal to voters but also to determine who could vote. The main issue was Florida's unusually strict felon-disenfranchisement law, which stripped the right to vote from all convicted felons even after the completion of their sentences and gave the Governor, and a Clemency Board under his oversight, basically unlimited discretion over how or whether to restore those rights. In 2011, Republican governor Rick Scott tightened restrictions, forcing convicted felons to wait a minimum of five years after sentence completion before they could apply to have their voting rights restored, restarting the five-year clock in the case of any misdemeanor arrests, and making it harder to get waivers. The Brennan Center for Justice reported that "in the period between 2010 and 2016, the disenfranchised population [of] Floridians grew by nearly 150,000 to a staggering estimated total of 1,686,000." In early 2018, a federal district court judge ruled that the voting restoration policy violated the First and Fourteenth Amendments, but that case was appealed to a higher court[11] and the felon voting ban was still in place on Election Day, when Gillum lost to DeSantis by fewer than 35,000 votes, or 0.4 per cent of the permitted vote.[12]

But in that same election, Florida voters approved an amendment to the state constitution which automatically restores the voting rights of Floridians who have finished serving their sentences for felonies other than murder or sexual crimes. This meant that 1.4 million individuals with prior convictions on their records became eligible to vote[13] ... or so it appeared. In March 2019, Republicans on a panel in the state House approved a proposal that would bar former felons from voting unless they fully paid court costs and administrative fees—which can be prohibitively expensive for poorer Floridians—and the Republican-controlled legislature appeared poised to take up that proposal.[14] Proponents of the measure said that it simply provides necessary clarifications and uniform criteria. Opponents described it rather differently. Democratic representative Adam Hattersley called it "blatantly unconstitutional as a poll tax,"[15] and Andrew Gillum said, "putting a price on restoring civil rights is unconstitutional and wrong."[16]

In both states, the arguments about constitutionality and justice have played out in the public square, at the ballot box, and also in the courts. It's worth taking a closer look at the history and implications of Georgia's and Florida's laws.

Georgia on My Mind

Georgia was the first state to approve a "poll tax," a fee charged to pro-spective voters, in 1871. Over the course of 20 years, Georgia increased those fees, added literacy tests and understanding tests, and ruled that only white people could vote in the Democratic primary (this was in the era when the Republican Party was still strongly associated with Lincoln in Southern minds, and when the Democratic nominee could be relied on to win most general elections).[17] Across the South, tests were administered selectively and often used specifically to disen-franchise black voters. This could be partly explained by the fact that during slavery it had in many places been illegal for a slave to learn to read, so the black population of former slave states was at a dis-advantage in terms of literacy; but even black college graduates were sometimes turned away for being unable to satisfy arbitrary "knowl-edge tests" that might require them to recite large portions of the Constitution from memory—tests not administered to white voters.[18]

In 1945, the Georgia legislature abolished the poll tax, and in 1947 the white primary rule was discarded, but the literacy test—and the hostility of some poll workers—still shut out many black voters. Just before the passage of the 1965 *Voting Rights Act* (*VRA*), fewer than 28 per cent of Georgia's nonwhite citizens of voting age were registered to vote, while more than 62 per cent of voting-age whites were registered.

This was clearly not due to political apathy on the part of non-white Georgians. Two years after the *VRA* passed, mandating fed-eral oversight of elections in states that were shown by various met-rics to practice race-based restriction of the franchise, 57 per cent of Georgia's eligible nonwhite citizens had registered to vote. By 2004, 66 per cent of black voting-age Georgians had registered, as had 74 per cent of whites.[19]

After the Supreme Court's 2013 decision to roll back *VRA* protec-tions (as discussed in my previous book),[20] Georgia was one of the states that took active steps to purge its voter rolls. Some 1.5 million vot-ers were cut from the rolls between the 2012 and 2016 elections—twice the number removed in the previous election cycle. Stacey Abrams's New Georgia Project and the NAACP fought these changes in court. In 2014 they backed a suit on behalf of more than 40,000 Georgians whose voter registrations had been lost, denied, or marked as "pending" because their identifying information didn't exactly match that given in the databases of Social Security or the Department of Driver Services; mismatches might be caused by confusion over hyphenated last names, or by mistakes made by local officials in entering voter registration information. Judge Christopher Brasher of the Fulton County Superior Court noted that many of the applicants represented in the suit were "underrepresented"—weren't white, or were young, or were first-time voters—but he said that "there has been no failure of a clear legal duty," and he ruled in favor of the state. Abrams vowed that the legal battle wasn't over.[21]

She was right about that. More lawsuits were brought. In 2016 the Georgia State Conference of the NAACP, Asian-Americans for Justice, and others challenged Brian Kemp's policy of automatically rejecting any voter application which showed any discrepancy in spaces, hyphens, etc., with other state records. Between 2013 and 2016, almost 35,000 registrations were denied or set to "pending" for this reason—and 64 per cent of those blocked registrations came from black voters. "That," McClatchy News reported, "made blacks eight times more likely than whites to have their voter registrations blocked or delayed because of the requirement ... [while] Asian-Americans and Latinos were more than six times as likely as white voters to have their applications halted." Just before a court hearing in September 2016, Kemp agreed to set aside the policy until the suit was resolved and to let voters whose applications had been blocked after 2015 vote in the 2016 election.[22]

In February 2017, the case was settled out of court and the exact-match policy was suspended. A spokesperson for Kemp told reporters, "Based on the advice of the Attorney General's office and in order to avoid the expense of further litigation, we agreed to settle this lawsuit." But she added, "The verification system Georgia had in place is important to accurately maintain our voter rolls and prevent illegal votes from being cast in our state's elections."[23] And, in May 2017, the Georgia legislature passed an exact-match law essentially reinstating the policy that Kemp had finally agreed to drop.[24]

The exact-match law was only part of Kemp's campaign—against voter fraud, according to him; against minority voters, according to his opponents. In July, Kemp oversaw a purge of the voter rolls which removed more than 500,000 people, or 8 per cent of the state's registered voters.[25] More than 107,000 of these removals happened simply because the voter had not voted for several election cycles.[26] The *Atlanta Journal-Constitution* noted that "more than 130,000 of those purged last year had registered to vote in 2008, the year of Barack Obama's historic presidential candidacy. Nearly half were minorities."[27]

In 2018, when Kemp, the crusader against voter fraud, and Abrams, the crusader for voting rights, faced each other on the campaign trail instead of in court, news broke that more than 53,000 voter registrations were still marked as "pending" by Kemp's office, mostly over exact-match issues. The AP investigated and found that, while Georgia's population was about 32-per-cent black, the pending voter registrations were nearly 70-per-cent black.[28]

Kemp was quick to explain that this was not a sign of racial animus or any wrongdoing on his part, but that his opponent and her supporters were to blame. He said that Abrams's New Georgia Project, which focused on registering minority voters, had done sloppy work, for which he couldn't be blamed.[29] Kemp had already investigated the New Georgia Project, beginning in 2014, alleging that they had committed voter fraud; that investigation wound down in 2017, as a total of 53 allegedly potentially fraudulent ballots were referred to the Georgia Attorney General, while the investigators conceded that they had no evidence of conspiracy by the New Georgia Project's leaders.[30] But on the campaign trail Kemp continued to accuse Abrams of supporting fraud, tweeting at one point that "Abrams wants illegal immigrants to choose our next governor." Abrams, meanwhile, accused Kemp of wanting to steal the votes of 53,000 Georgians.[31] Both sides dug in for a long and bitter fight on the airwaves and in the courts.

On 2 November, US District Judge Eleanor Ross ruled against the exact-match voter registration policy, saying it raised "grave concerns for the Court about the differential treatment inflicted on a group of individuals who are predominantly minorities.... The election scheme here places a severe burden on these individuals." She ordered that poll managers must be allowed to clear voters who showed proof of citizenship, and she required Kemp to issue a news release explaining how that could be done. News stories said this could restore voting rights to 3,000 people—far short of the number disenfranchised under Kemp.[32] Four days later, on election night, Kemp took the lead in the vote, but Abrams refused to concede and waited for the status of provisional ballots to be determined.

Less than a week after the election, a federal judge delayed certification of Georgia's election results, noting that "repeated inaccuracies were identified in the voter registration system that caused qualified voters likely to lose their vote or to be channeled at best into the provisional voting process because their registration records did not appear or had been purged from the data system," and "certain counties and precincts stintingly provided provisional ballots to voters despite the volume of individuals facing registration issues at the polls." Abrams's supporters hailed this decision as an acknowledgement of injustice; Kemp's spokesman spoke bitterly of liberals attempting to steal an election they could not win.[33] A few days later, Abrams acknowledged that Kemp was Georgia's governor but said he had stolen the election.

Abrams's accusation is still being weighed in the courts and by the US House. Questioned about the House investigation, Kemp dismissed it as "playing politics" and went on to complain about Democrats being "hung up on giving more money to Puerto Rico when we have our own farmers who are fixing to lose their farm.... I would urge them to do the real work of this country. Take care of the people who need relief."[34]

This may not be a non sequitur after all. Puerto Ricans are also American citizens and are already struggling with the aftermath of a deadly hurricane and a disproportionately ill-funded recovery. Why are they not seen as "our own" and "need[ing] relief"? Does the answer have anything to do with their ethnicity, and, if so, does this shed any light on which Georgian citizens Kemp might understand himself to be representing?

Georgia legislators do seem to agree that something needs to be done about elections, but they don't agree about what that might be. Republicans are backing a push for touch-screen voting machines. Democrats are trying to make voter registration easier and to end the voter-purge system—but since they don't control the legislature (and, some might say, are unlikely to control the legislature so long as the present voter-registration regime stands), no one seems to believe that state-government–led change is coming any time soon.[35] But Abrams's voting rights group Fair Fight Action continues to challenge Kemp in the courts (and to face its own legal challenges)[36] and to encourage voter registration.[37]

Florida Man

While the Georgia electoral controversy was based on a somewhat arcane and tangled set of rules, the main Florida controversy over voter eligibility seemed to stem from one clear and straightforward state law: the state constitution's denial of voting rights to felons, along with the laws making restoration subject to the discretion of the Governor and his Clemency Board. But even this apparently straightforward law has a tangled history.

Florida's 1838 constitution specified that "the General Assembly shall have power to exclude from every office of honor, trust or profit, within the State, and from the right of suffrage, all persons convicted of bribery, perjury, or other infamous crime."[38] In 1868, soon after the Civil War ended, the Constitution stated that "no person under guardianship *non compos mentis*, or insane, shall be qualified to vote at any election, nor shall any person convicted of felony be qualified to vote at any election unless restored to civil rights."[39] Now, to some Floridians this sounds like a simple and race-blind provision keeping people who have committed particularly heinous crimes from voting. But a closer look raises some questions.

First of all, while the popular imagination of felonies is likely to feature murder, rape, and child molestation, it appears that the majority of Floridians disenfranchised for felony convictions have not in fact committed such crimes. As stated above, the Brennan Center for Justice estimated that approximately 1,686,000 Floridians were disenfranchised for felony convictions in 2016, and the 2018 measure restoring the franchise to felons who had completed their sentences specifically excluded those convicted of murder or felony sex crimes and yet re-enfranchised 1.4 million people, or the vast majority of the disenfranchised.[40] Floridians can receive felony convictions for such offenses as auto theft, carrying a handgun without permission, and selling marijuana to a minor.[41] Should such offenses strip a citizen of voting rights in perpetuity?

Second, as discussed in my previous book, black Americans are treated more harshly than their white fellow citizens at every stage of our so-called criminal justice system. Florida is no exception. The ACLU reported that in Florida, black motorists were nearly as likely as white motorists to wear seat belts (85.8 per cent for blacks, 91.5 per cent for whites) but were twice as likely to be stopped and ticketed for seat-belt violations. The ACLU pointed out that such apparently minor stops are not always trivial in their consequences: "Sam Dubose. Walter Scott. Sandra Bland. 2015 showed in terrible and vivid detail how even routine police traffic stops carry the risk of escalating to arrest or the use of force—even lethal force. Traffic stops are not simply innocuous encounters. They can be deadly, particularly for Black people."[42] These disparities extend to sentencing. A 2016 tri-county survey in Florida found that black defendants received sentences for drug dealing and battery that were twice as long as those of white defendants with identical charges and similar backgrounds. It also found that white defendants were more likely to be offered plea deals and chances to scrub felony charges.[43]

This implies that felony disenfranchisement would disproportionately disenfranchise black voters, even if records were kept accurately. But in 2018 the bipartisan US Commission on Civil Rights reported, "From 2000–2012, Florida was repeatedly charged with allegations that it engaged in systemic purges impacting voters of color. This is a subject that the Commission examined in the 2000 report *Voting Irregularities in Florida during the 2000 Presidential Election*, which after careful examination of purges of voters in Florida found that both the method of the purge and its outcome directly and negatively affected black voters. Moreover, the Commission found credible evidence that "the human consequences" of Florida's 2000 voter-purge program, which was based on inaccurate data about alleged felony convictions, were severe and disparately impacted black voters. The Commission also found that most voters who were removed were in fact eligible, that "countless" Floridians were denied their right to vote, and that "disenfranchisement of Florida voters fell most harshly on the shoulders of African Americans."[44] In the next presidential election cycle, in 2004, Florida conducted an extremely similar purge targeting persons with felony convictions with a reported discriminatory impact on black voters.[45]

In recent years, concerns have been raised about the additional potential for injustice raised by a highly arbitrary system of re-enfranchisement. In 2000 the Brennan Center for Restorative Justice filed suit on behalf of more than 60,000 disenfranchised Floridians, arguing that the permanent disenfranchisement policy had discriminatory intent and violated the Fourteenth and Fifteenth Amendment rights of Floridians. A federal district upheld the Florida policy; a panel from the 11th Circuit overturned it; the state appealed, and the entire 11th Circuit upheld it; and the Supreme Court declined to hear the case.[46]

In 2007 Governor Charlie Crist used his broad powers of discretion to automatically re-enfranchise people who had completed their sentences for certain nonviolent felonies, including low-level drug dealing; about 115,000 Floridians had their voting rights restored.[47] But in 2011 newly elected Governor Rick Scott pushed back those reforms and added new barriers to the restoration of voting rights.

A group of people who had completed felony convictions and been refused in their applications for the restoration of suffrage sued Governor Scott, backed by the Fair Elections Legal Network, and in February 2018, US District Judge Mark Walker gave a blistering ruling in favor of the plaintiffs.[48] In his ruling he objected vehemently to the arbitrary and potentially discriminatory nature of the re-enfranchisement process:

> Florida's Executive Clemency Board has, by rule, unfettered discretion in restoring voting rights. "We can do whatever we want," the Governor said at one clemency hearing.... One need not search long to find alarming illustrations of this scheme in action. In 2010, a white man, Steven Warner, cast an illegal ballot. Three years later, he sought the restoration of his voting rights. He went before the state's Executive Clemency Board, where Governor Scott asked him about his illegal voting. "Actually, I voted for you," he said. The Governor laughed. "I probably shouldn't respond to that." A few seconds passed. The Governor then granted the former felon his voting rights.... But Plaintiffs identify five former felons who, at other points, were questioned about illegal ballots cast and then rejected on that basis.... It is not lost on this Court that four of the five rejected applicants are African-American.[49]

Judge Walker also noted the prevalence of viewpoint discrimination:

> Plaintiffs identify several instances of former felons who professed political views amenable to the Board's members who then received

voting rights, while those who expressed contrary political views to the Board were denied those same rights. Applicants—as well as their character witnesses—have routinely invoked their conservative beliefs and values to their benefit.... Similar disparities arise when applicants criticize the system. For example, a Navy veteran decried felon disenfranchisement before the Governor rejected his application because of traffic infractions. Id. at 28–29. But ten former felons—who did not speak out against felony disenfranchisement—were re-enfranchised despite less-than-perfect traffic records.[50]

And he pointed out the racial gap in disenfranchisement: "More than one-tenth of Florida's voting population—nearly 1.7 million as of 2016—cannot vote because they have been decimated from the body politic. More than one in five of Florida's African American voting-age population cannot vote.... No more. When the risk of state-sanctioned viewpoint discrimination skulks near the franchise, it is the province and duty of this Court to excise such potential bias from infecting the clemency process."[51]

But the judge's decision was appealed, and 1.6 million Floridians were still disenfranchised when Ron DeSantis got nearly 34,000 more votes than Andrew Gillum in the general election. And, while most of those people were re-enfranchised by the voters on Election Day 2018, the Republicans elected while their votes couldn't be counted are now moving to block the re-enfranchisement of Floridians who haven't paid all their court administrative costs.[52]

Those costs can be considerable. The *Miami Herald* reported in the wake of the Republican fee-payment proposal that in Pinellas County anyone convicted of a felony will owe at least $413 in court fees (not restitution to victims, not fines imposed at sentencing, but administrative costs) and will probably have to pay at least an additional $150; many will owe over $1,000 in such costs.[53] This may sound like small potatoes to lawmakers, but a 2016 Federal Reserve survey found that 46 per cent of Americans said they did not have enough money to cover an unexpected expense of $400; within each income bracket, black Americans were more likely than whites to say they could not meet such an expense.[54] Given this, it is hardly surprising that numerous voter advocates have condemned the proposed fee requirement as a new poll tax.

Andrew Gillum, like Stacey Abrams, is staying involved with voting rights. His group, Bring It Home Florida, hopes to register and engage one million new voters before the 2020 elections. Gillum has also expressed his commitment to fighting the "poll tax" and making certain that people with prior felony convictions are actually allowed to vote, even if they are poor.[55]

The Rule, Not the Exception

Gutting of the federal *Voting Rights Act* by the US Supreme Court in 2013 has given some states a green light to enact voter-suppression tactics that may no longer get them in trouble with federal civil rights law. Section 5 of the *VRA* established that "jurisdictions with a history of discrimination must seek pre-approval of changes in voting rules that could affect minorities." This process, known as "preclearance," blocks discrimination before it occurs.[56] *Shelby County v. Holder*, 133 S. Ct. 2612 (2013) "held that it is unconstitutional to use the coverage formula in Section 4(b) of the Voting Rights Act to determine which jurisdictions are subject to the preclearance requirement of Section 5 of the Voting Rights Act."[57]

According to the United States Department of Justice, "The Supreme Court did not rule on the constitutionality of Section 5 itself. The effect of the Shelby County decision is that the jurisdictions identified by the coverage formula in Section 4(b) no longer need to seek preclearance for the new voting changes, unless they are covered by a separate court order entered under Section 3(c) of the Voting Rights Act."[58] Entire states previously covered by this preclearance rule include Alabama, Alaska, Georgia, Louisiana, Mississippi, South Carolina, Texas, and Virginia. Certain jurisdictions of Arizona, Hawaii, Idaho, and North Carolina were also covered. In the ensuing decades, jurisdictions in Alaska, Arizona, California, Connecticut, Florida, Idaho, Maine, Massachusetts, Michigan, New Hampshire, New York, South Dakota, and Wyoming were added to the preclearance list.

Shortly after the *Shelby* decision, many states hastily introduced and passed major changes to their voting laws and procedures. Recently, Georgia and Florida may have caught the nation's attention when it comes to voting rights, but they are hardly unique in their approach to suppressing the vote. In September 2018, the bipartisan US Commission on Civil Rights released its assessment of minority voting rights access and came unanimously to several troubling conclusions, including that in states across the country—and particularly in many previously covered under the preclearance requirements of the *VRA*—new laws and voting procedures are impacting minority voting rights (they list voter ID laws, closure of polling places, restriction of early voting, and voter roll purges) and "since *Shelby County* halted the federal preclearance regime, elections have taken place under laws that were later found in court to be intentionally discriminatory against communities of color."[59]

Among many other problematic practices, the Commission noted that New York and Ohio, as well as Georgia, have removed inactive voters from their rolls, with a disproportionate impact on communities of color.[60] Under the *National Voter Registration Act* (*NVRA*) of 1993, states are required to update voter rolls in a non-partisan and non-discriminatory way, but "because the NVRA does not restrict states from systematically cleaning voter lists during an election cycle, many have amended their election codes to require monthly voter list maintenance."[61] Many states have enacted controversial inactive voter–purge laws in the name of fair elections and combating voter fraud.[62]

The Supreme Court has decided that Ohio's process, considered the most stringent in the nation for removing inactive voters, is constitutional and in accordance with the *NVRA*, but civil rights groups argue the process disproportionately purges minority voters from the rolls. In her dissenting argument, Supreme Court Justice Sotomayor appeared to agree with civil rights groups citing data that found "in Hamilton County—which includes Cincinnati—African-American neighborhoods in the city had 10 percent of their voters removed due to inactivity, as compared to only 4 percent in the suburban, white-majority neighborhoods."[63] Under the challenged law, voters in Ohio who miss a single federal election are flagged to receive a confirmation notice, and if they fail to respond to that notice (or engage in other defined activities) in the next four years, they are removed from the voter rolls.[64]

ID Requirements

Newly enacted voter ID laws that affect registration as well as voting have invoked controversy and confusion across the country. The *Help America Vote Act (HAVA)* of 2002 instituted a "limited" identification requirement for persons who register to vote by mail and have "not previously voted in a federal election in the jurisdiction.... They must provide a current, valid photo ID or a copy of a current utility bill, bank statement, government check, paycheck, or other government document with [their] name and address, whether voting in person or by mail."[65] Voters who register while renewing or obtaining a license from a DMV are exempt from this requirement since they are already providing documentation to obtain the license. While a majority of states do have ID requirements (some accept non-photo IDs), the ACLU argues that strict photo voter ID laws disproportionately burden specific demographics of voters, including students, the elderly, people living in rural areas, people of color, and low-income people.[66]

The ACLU, researchers, and civil rights groups have found that obtaining a government-issued photo ID is an undue burden for many voters in the aforementioned groups due to the cost and burden of obtaining documents, such as birth certificates, needed to apply for government-issued identification. Many members of these groups also lack the time to obtain documents to apply for an ID or may lack transportation to government offices. While drivers' licenses are an acceptable form of photo ID in strict photo ID–requirement states, it has been found that people of color are less likely than whites to have a driver's license.[67]

Some states have tried to circumvent the cost argument by providing voter identification certificates free of cost; however, applicants must still pay fees to obtain documents needed to apply for the certificates. For example, in Texas, "Election Identification Certificates" can be obtained free of cost, but few voters without an acceptable government ID actually obtain these certificates. Furthermore, many elections administrators are not even aware that such a certificate exists or that it can be substituted for a photo ID.[68]

In several states as well, Hispanic voters have felt intimidated by requirements to prove their citizenship. A case was brought by the ACLU on behalf of Kansas voters, alleging that the state was not in compliance with the *NVRA* when they asked Kansans applying for or renewing their drivers license to produce documentary proof of citizenship.[69] States that require documentary proof of citizenship have been challenged in court, with some litigation still pending.

Students are a highly mobile population that also relies disproportionately on public transportation, and they too are less likely to have driver's licenses and other forms of government issued ID.[70] Furthermore, multiple localities and states have challenged students' right to vote based on the premise that they are not permanent residents of their college towns, even though some students live year-round on campus. These challenges to student voting rights have sparked legal challenges and advocacy around the country for many years.

There also have been lawsuits alleging that government offices did not properly educate the public about identification needed to vote. For example, in Wisconsin in 2016 a district court found that DMV offices were not providing enough accurate information about the type of IDs that citizens needed in order to vote.[71]

In several states there has been confusion about whether student IDs are an acceptable form of identification for voting. In Texas, student IDs are not an acceptable form of identification to vote. Wisconsin allows student IDs, but not if they are "expired" or unsigned.[72] Furthermore, Virginia at one time did not accept private-college ID cards as valid forms of identification until this rule was struck down in the state courts.[73]

For some Historically Black College and Universities, the struggle for voting rights dates back to the enactment of the *Voting Rights Act*. Students at Prairie View A&M University, for example, have been fighting for their right to vote for decades. The Waller County elections administrators argued back in the early 1970s that students needed to be on the property-tax rolls to be considered residents of the county. The case went to the Supreme Court and the students won their right to vote.[74] Fast forward to 2018, and the students were fighting the county to have the same number of early voting hours afforded to predominantly white communities in the state. The campus polling-location hours had been limited to workday hours, which the students argued inconvenienced working students. In addition, according to the *Texas Tribune*, "thousands of students who live on campus at Prairie View A&M had been incorrectly told to register to vote using an address in a different precinct and would need to fill out a change-of-address form before casting a ballot."[75]

Other Tactics

Early voting, a tool proven to increase minority voting,[76] has been curtailed in several states, including Florida, Georgia, Indiana, Nebraska, North Carolina, Ohio, Tennessee, and Wisconsin.[77] Shortly after *Shelby*, for example, North Carolina's Republican-led legislature voted to eliminate an entire week from early voting, but this change was struck down by the Fourth Circuit Court of Appeals. In this case, the state quite candidly admitted that it wanted to eliminate Sunday voting because it increased minority voting, and African-American citizens tend to vote Democratic. In this case, it was discovered that the legislature had "requested and utilized racial data, including a breakdown by race of DMV issued ID ownership, absentee and early voting, and same day registration" to analyze whether African Americans disproportionately used these voting tools. In North Carolina's case, the discriminatory motive for changing the laws was obviously there.

Eliminating polling places has been another voter-suppression tool used in Republican-led states. After the *Shelby* decision, certain states formerly required to get federal preclearance under the *VRA*, including Alabama, Arizona, Louisiana, Mississippi, North Carolina, South Carolina, and Texas, cut the number of polling places, sometimes with a clearly disproportionate impact on minority voters.[78] Over the past decade, news organization have reported on long lines and wait times to vote in many large cities in the US. Waits can surpass six hours, with some voters waiting in very hot weather for their chance to vote. While many elections agencies argue that they must cut early and absentee voting to save money on operations and staff, these changes sow confusion and aggravation.[79]

States with Republican control of both the executive and legislative branches have led the way in disenfranchising minority voters since *Shelby*. Table 2.1 illustrates that most of the problematic laws passed since 2012 have been passed by Republican-controlled state legislatures. Although some Democratic states have also enacted several questionable measures, the breadth of voter-suppression measures that Republican states have enacted is quite striking.

TABLE 2.1
Summary of voting rights barriers in the states

State	Legislative branch party control (2019)[i]	Strict photo ID requirement/ Follow-up needed if no ID[ii]	No automatic restoration of voting rights for felons[iii]
New registration/Voting restrictions enacted since 2012 (does not include new ID requirements)[iv]			
Alabama	Republican		X
Proof of citizenship required when registering to vote using national voter registration (ongoing litigation)			
Alaska	Republican		
Arizona	Republican		X
Felony to collect and deliver mail-in ballots (exception for family members, caregivers, and postal-service employees)			
Arkansas	Republican		
California	Democratic		
Colorado	Democratic		
Connecticut	Democratic		
Delaware	Democratic		X
District of Columbia	Democratic		
Florida	Republican		X
Shortened early voting period, curtailed voter registration drives			
Georgia	Republican	X	
Voters prevented from voting if registration information was not an exact match to information in other state records, reduced early voting period and eliminated voting weekend before Election Day, proof of citizenship required when registering to vote using national voter registration			
Hawaii	Democratic		
Idaho	Republican		
Illinois	Republican		
Curtailed voter-registration drives			
Indiana	Republican	X	
Flawed voter-purge procedures enacted that currently are not in effect due to a preliminary injunction			

Iowa	Republican		X
Curtailed voter-registration drives, increased requirements for same-day registration and early and absentee voting			
Kansas	Republican	X	
Proof of citizenship documents required to register using the state voter registration form			
Kentucky	Republican		X
Louisiana	Republican		
Maine	Democratic		
Maryland	Democratic		
Massachusetts	Democratic		
Michigan	Republican		
Minnesota	Split		
Mississippi	Republican	X	X
Missouri	Republican		
Montana	Republican		
Civic groups and individuals (with certain exceptions) cannot assist with absentee voting by collecting and delivering ballots			
Nebraska	Nonpartisan		X
Shortened early voting period			
Nevada	Democratic		X
New Hampshire	Democratic		
Tougher requirements for students registering to vote			
New Jersey	Democratic		
New Mexico	Democratic		
New York	Republican		
North Carolina	Republican		
Implemented uniform early voting hours across the state (this tends to reduce voting in larger cities), eliminated early voting last Saturday before election			
North Dakota	Republican		
Ohio	Republican		
Shortened early voting period, eliminated same-time registration and voting "week," changed absentee and provisional ballot rules (court challenges continuing)			
Oklahoma	Republican		
Oregon	Democratic		
Pennsylvania	Republican		
Rhode Island	Democratic		
South Carolina	Republican		
South Dakota	Republican		X

Tennessee	Republican	X	X
Proof of citizenship required for certain flagged individuals, shortened early voting period			
Texas	Republican		
Voter-registration drives curtailed			
Utah	Republican		
Vermont	Democratic		
Virginia	Republican	X	X
Groups that hold voter-registration drives must register with the state, forms must be returned within 10 days			
Washington	Democratic		
West Virginia	Republican		
Shortened early voting period			
Wisconsin	Republican	X	X
Cut hours for early voting during week and eliminated hours completely on weekends under the guise of instituting uniform voting hours across the states, effectively reduced in-person absentee voting in cities, change is still being litigated in court			
Wyoming	Republican		X

i   Alan Greenblatt, "All or Nothing," in *Governing the States and Localities*, https://www.governing.com/topics/politics/gov-state-politics-governors-2019.html.

ii   See National Conference of State Legislatures, "Felon Voting Rights," 21 December 2018, http://www.ncsl.org/research/elections-and-campaigns/felon-voting-rights.aspx.

iii   Ibid. This is the harshest scenario in regard to the loss and restoration of voting rights for felons. Felons in Maine and Vermont never lose their voting rights, while in the remaining states there is automatic restoration after completion of their sentence, and in some states, parole/probation. For additional information for Florida, see Veronica Stracqualursi and Caroline Kelly, "Florida House Passes Bill That Makes It Harder for Ex-Felons to Vote," *CNN*, 3 May 2019.

iv   See Brennan Center for Justice, "New Voting Restrictions in America." For additional information for Wisconsin, see Laurel White, "Wisconsin Supreme Court Sides with GOP Lawmakers to Limit Democratic Governor's Power," *NPR*, 21 June 2019, https://www.npr.org/2019/06/21/734722467/wisconsin-supreme-court-sides-with-gop-lawmakers-to-limit-democratic-governors-p.

In some states, including Arkansas, North Carolina, and Texas, new ID laws and changes to other voting procedures have been found to be discriminatory, while laws passed in other states have been upheld. New voting laws are often enacted with the public, and even elections administrators and staff, not thoroughly understanding the new rules.[80] This results in confusion when citizens register, and on Election Day, with the end result being disenfranchisement for many voters. Some voters persist, however, and may even file lawsuits. Advocates are learning and helping every step of the way. For example, civil rights organizations have learned that the combined effects of new voting laws passed by a state must be challenged rather than litigating each measure separately.[81]

Despite some wins and reversals across the country, the overall effect of the *Shelby* case on voting rights has been troubling. Since the Supreme Court's ruling, the US Commission on Civil Rights unanimously called on Congress to strengthen the *VRA* and "restore and expand protections against discrimination, including federal preclearance."[82]

Gerrymandered Congressional Districts

Gerrymandering is a vital tool in an era of bad-faith politics where intentionally discriminatory acts are shrouded in a cloak of fairness. Conservatives draw Congressional districts that are gerrymandered to concentrate minority voters into Democratic districts and white Republican voters into conservative districts. It is argued that the party in power has legitimate authority to draw district lines to their advantage, but gerrymandered districts are far from good faith politics. In fact, gerrymandering in itself is a necessary tool of bad faith. Without diverse districts, minority voters' voices are diluted, while the democratic process is presented as legitimate and fair.

Even when black voters are allowed to register and are able to cast their ballots, gerrymandered districts can effectively restrict their political power. Political parties that control both houses of their state legislative branch have great power in redrawing state and federal legislative districts after each census. Some states have special commissions that either advise the legislative branch on redistricting or take on most of the redistricting work directly.[83]

North Carolina is a case in point of how one party can create leg-islative districts to benefit them electorally. In 2016, Republican law-makers redrew district lines. In the 2018 elections, Democratic House candidates received 48 per cent of the votes cast but won only three of thirteen Congressional seats.[84] The redistricting was avowedly a partisan gerrymander; as the *New York Times* reports, "The map has a 10-3 Republican tilt, one of its drafters said 'because I do not believe it's possible to draw a map with 11 Republicans and two Democrats.'" But, given the strong racial tinge of partisan politics, political gerry-manders may often become racial gerrymanders. One North Carolina district boundary deviates from its line to cut, not only through the middle of the mostly Democratic city of Greensboro but also through the middle of the nation's largest historically black university. A stu-dent assigned a dorm change had to re-register to vote, having become a constituent of a different district.[85]

The Supreme Court is now considering this case, along with a case of pro-Democratic gerrymandering in Maryland. In 2017 the court struck down North Carolina's drawing of two congressional districts on the grounds that the boundaries had been drawn in a way that was racially motivated without proper cause,[86] and that earlier decision may be a relevant precedent for the partisan gerrymandering cases coming forward today.

Pennsylvania provides another recent case that has garnered national attention. Republicans sought to keep gerrymandered dis-tricts that had been used since 2011. In arguing that gerrymandered districts diluted the vote for the opposition party in Pennsylvania, the American Bar Association cited these facts: "In the three elections since its adoption, Republicans won the same 13 districts each cycle while Democrats won only five, despite the fact that Republicans received, at most, 55 percent of the vote. In 2012, Democrats won a majority of the vote across the state, but again won only 5 out of 18 seats."[87] Eighteen citizens brought a lawsuit arguing that the cur-rent districts violated their rights guaranteed by the state constitu-tion, including the Pennsylvania Constitution's Free Expression and Association Clauses, as well as its Equal Protection guarantees and the Free and Equal Clause.[88]

In 2018 Pennsylvania's highest court struck down the Republicans' federal congressional redistricting map, finding it violated the state's constitution. The case made its way up to the Supreme Court, which failed to reverse the state court's ruling. As part of its ruling, the Pennsylvania court created its own redistricting map that the state legislature was required to follow in drawing up new Congressional districts.[89]

Notes

1   Thomas Wheatley, "Georgia Is Moving in Democrats' Direction. For Stacey Abrams, Will It Be Fast Enough?" *Atlanta Magazine*, 2 October 2018.

2   Grace Segers, "Who Is Stacey Abrams?," *CBS News*, 5 February 2019.

3   Sarah Totonchi and Marissa Hall Dodgson, "Criminal Justice Reform in Georgia Cannot End with Governor Deal," *Atlanta Magazine*, 24 September 2018, 9.

4   Griffin Connolly, "Georgia Gov. Brian Kemp Brushes Off House Investigation of Voter Suppression," *Roll Call*, 6 March 2019.

5   Alana Semuels, "Reverse Migration Might Turn Georgia Blue," *The Atlantic*, 23 May 2018.

6   Jenny Jarvie, "Voting Rights Activists File Major Federal Lawsuit against Georgia Election Officials," *Los Angeles Times*, 27 November 2018.

7   Connolly, "Georgia Gov. Brian Kemp Brushes Off House Investigation of Voter Suppression."

8   Kristina Torres, "Georgia AG Gets 53 Forms in Fraud Probe of Stacey Abrams' Voter Registration Group," *Atlanta Journal and Constitution*, 20 September 2017.

9   "Full Text: Stacey Abrams' Speech to End the Georgia Governor's Race," *11 Alive*, https://www.11alive.com/article/news/politics/elections/full-text-stacey-abrams-speech-to-end-the-georgia-governors-race/85-96949a83-c2ed-4467-929e-2794f43afa23.

10   Andrew Gillum, "*On The Issues* Position Summary: On Civil Rights," September 2017, www.ontheissues.org/Andrew_Gillum.htm.

11   Brennan Center for Justice, "Voting Rights Restoration Efforts in Florida," 31 May 2019, https://www.brennancenter.org/our-work/research-reports/voting-rights-restoration-efforts-florida.

12   "Florida Election Results 2018," *Politico*, 27 August 2019.

13   Brennan Center for Justice, "Voting Rights."

14   *New York Times* Editorial Board, "The Return of the Poll Tax in Florida," 22 March 2019.

15 Karen Zraick, "Florida Republicans Push to Make Ex-Felons Pay Fees before They Can Vote," *New York Times*, 20 March 2019.

16 *New York Times Editorial Board*, "Return."

17 Charles S. Bullock III and Ronald Keith Gaddie, "Voting Rights Progress in Georgia," *N.Y.U. Journal of Legislation and Public Policy* 10.1 (2006): 1–49.

18 "Voting Rights Act of 1965," 6 June 2019, https://www.history.com/topics/black-history/voting-rights-act.

19 Bullock and Gaddie, "Voting Rights Progress in Georgia."

20 Bailey, *Racial Realities*, 63.

21 Kristina Torres, "Georgia Judge Sides with State in 'Missing' Voters Case," *Atlanta Journal-Constitution*, 29 October 2014.

22 Tony Pugh, "Georgia Secretary of State Fighting Accusations of Disenfranchising Minority Voters," *McClatchy News*, 7 October 2016.

23 Kristina Torres, "Georgia Settles Federal Lawsuit Alleging It Blocked Thousands of Minority Voters," *Atlanta Journal-Constitution*, 9 February 2017.

24 HB 268, 2017–2018 Regular Session of the Georgia General Assembly, http://www.legis.ga.gov/Legislation/en-US/display/20172018/HB/268.

25 Alan Judd, "Georgia's Strict Laws Lead to Large Purge of Voters," *Atlanta Journal-Constitution*, 27 October 2018.

26 Angela Caputo, Geoff Hing, and Johnny Kauffman, "They Didn't Vote.... Now They Can't," *American Public Media*, 19 October 2018.

27 Judd, "Georgia's Strict Laws."

28 Ben Nadler, "Voting Rights Become a Flashpoint in Georgia Governor's Race," *AP News*, 9 October 2018.

29 Ibid.

30 Torres, "Georgia AG Gets 53 Forms in Fraud Probe of Stacey Abrams' Voter Registration Group."

31 Amy Gardner and Vanessa Williams, "In Georgia, Governor's Race Evokes Old Tensions over Voting and Race," *Washington Post*, 19 October 2018.

32 Shannon Van Sant, "Judge Rules against Georgia Election Law, Calling It a 'Severe Burden' for Voters," *NPR*, 3 November 2018.

33 Alan Blinder, "Federal Judge Delays Certification of Georgia Election Results," *New York Times*, 12 November 2018.

34 Griffin Connolly, "Georgia Gov. Brian Kemp Brushes Off House Investigation of Voter Suppression," *Roll Call*, 6 March 2019, http://www.rollcall.com/news/congress/house-democrats-investigating-georgia-gov-brian-kemp-for-voter-suppression.

35   David Lightman and Maggie Lee, "House Democrats Pass Bill to Make Voter Purges Harder," *McClatchy News*, 8 March 2019.

36   "Is Abrams' Nonprofit Fighting for Voter Rights or Just Her Career? Spending Will Determine," *MSN*, 21 March 2019.

37   Emma Newberger, "Stacey Abrams, after Narrow Election Loss, Vows to Fight for Voter Rights," *CNBC*, 8 March 2019.

38   Florida Constitution of 1838, Article VI, section 4, https://constitution.com/florida-state-constitution-1838/.

39   Ibid.

40   Brennan Center for Justice, "Voting Rights."

41   Ave Mince-Didier, "Florida Felony Crimes by Class and Sentence," *Nolo*, https://www.criminaldefenselawyer.com/resources/criminal-defense/state-felony-laws/florida-felony-class.htm.

42   Nusrat Choudhury, "New Evidence Suggesting Racial Profiling on Florida Roadways," *ACLU Florida*, 27 January 2016.

43   Josh Salman, Emily Le Coz, and Elizabeth Johnson, "Florida's Broken Sentencing System," *Herald Tribune*, 12 December 2016.

44   "Voting Irregularities in Florida during the 2000 Presidential Election," Chapter 9: Findings and Recommendations, https://www.usccr.gov/pubs/vote2000/report/ch9.htm.

45   US Commission on Civil Rights, *An Assessment of Minority Voting Rights Access in the United States*, Statutory Report 2018, 145–46.

46   Brennan Center for Justice, "Johnson v. Bush," 14 November 2005, https://www.brennancenter.org/our-work/court-cases/johnson-v-bush.

47   Kahlil Williams, "FL: Still Much Work to Be Done," Brennan Center for Justice, 20 June 2008, https://casetext.com/analysis/fl-still-much-work-to-be-done.

48   Derek Hawkins, "Florida's Ban on Ex-Felons Voting Is Unconstitutional and Biased, Federal Judge Rules," *Washington Post*, 2 February 2018.

49   Mark E. Walker, "Order on Cross-Motions for Summary Judgment," February 1, 2018, US District Court, Northern District of Florida, Tallahassee Division.

50   Ibid.

51   Ibid.

52   *New York Times* Editorial Board, "The Return of the Poll Tax in Florida."

53   Lawrence Mower and David Ovalle, "How Much Will Regaining the Right to Vote Cost Florida Felons? It Could Be a Lot," *Miami Herald*, 21 March 2019.

54   Ylan Q. Mui, "The Shocking Number of Americans Who Can't Cover a $400 Expense," *Washington Post*, 25 May 2016.

55   Daniel Rivero, "Andrew Gillum Lays Out Plan to Register Voters across Florida," *WLRN*, 20 March 2019.

56   United States Department of Justice, *About Section 5 of the* Voting Rights Act, https://www.justice.gov/crt/about-section-5-voting-rights-act.

57   Ibid.

58   Ibid.

59   United States Commission on Civil Rights, "U.S. Commission on Civil Rights Releases Report: *An Assessment of Minority Voting Rights Access in the United States*," Press Release, 12 September 2018, https://www.usccr.gov/press/2018/09-12-18-PR.pdf.

60   US Commission on Civil Rights, *Assessment*, 154.

61   Thessalia Merivaki and Sean Conner, "Managing Voter Registration Lists the Hybrid Way: The Case of Mississippi," *Mississippi State University Working Paper Prepared for the 2018 Election Sciences, Reform and Administration Conference*, Madison, WI, 25–27 July 2018.

62   Erin A. Penrod, "Disenfranchisement 2.0: Recent Voter ID Laws and the Implications Thereof," *U. St. Thomas Law Journal* 14.1 (2018): 207.

63   Nina Totenberg, "Supreme Court Upholds Controversial Ohio Voter-Purge Law," *NPR*, 11 June 2018.

64   Brennan Center for Justice, "Husted v. A. Philip Randolph Institute," 11 June 2018,https://www.brennancenter.org/our-work/court-cases/husted-v-philip-randolph-institute.

65   Eric A. Fischer, R. Sam Garrett, and L. Paige Whitaker, "State Voter Identification Requirements: Analysis, Legal Issues, and Policy Considerations," Congressional Research Service, 21 October 2016, 2, fas.org/sgp/crs/misc/R42806.pdf.

66   ACLU, "Oppose Voter ID Legislation—Fact Sheet," May 2017, https://www.aclu.org/other/oppose-voter-id-legislation-fact-sheet.

67   John Pawasarat and Lois M. Quinn, *ETI Research on Disparate Racial Impacts of Using Driver's Licenses for Voter IDs* (University of Wisconsin Milwaukee: ETI Publications, 2017), https://dc.uwm.edu/cgi/viewcontent.cgi?article=1184&context=eti_pubs.

68   Ibid.

69   ACLU Kansas, "Federal Judge Rules in Favor of ACLU, Strikes Down Kobach's Illegal Voter Restrictions," 18 June 2018, https://www.aclukansas.org/en/news/federal-judge-rules-favor-aclu-strikes-down-kobachs-illegal-voter-restrictions.

70   Penrod, "Disenfranchisement 2.0."

71   Richard L. Hasen, "Softening Voter ID Laws through Litigation: Is It Enough?," *Wisconsin Law Review*, 20 September 2016.

72   Litigation is still pending. Brennan Center for Justice, "New Voting
     Restrictions in America," 1 October 2019, https://www.brennancenter.org/
     our-work/research-reports/new-voting-restrictions-america.

73   Ibid.

74   Vann R. Newkirk II and Adam Harris, "Fighting for the Right to Vote in a
     Tiny Texas County," *The Atlantic*, 1 November 2018.

75   Matt Zdun, "Prairie View A&M University's Voter Registration Issues Are
     Resolved, but Voting Barriers Remain," *Texas Tribune*, 16 October 2018.

76   Penrod, "Disenfranchisement 2.0"; Fisher et al., "State Voter Identification
     Requirements."

77   US Commission on Civil Rights, *Assessment*, 158.

78   Ibid., 170.

79   Mark Nichols, "Closed Voting Sites Hit Minority Counties Harder for Busy
     Midterm Elections," *USA Today*, 20 October 2018.

80   Fisher et al., "State Voter Identification Requirements."

81   Penrod, "Disenfranchisement 2.0."

82   "U.S. Commission on Civil Rights Releases Report: An Assessment of
     Minority Voting Rights Access in the United States," *PR Newswire*, 12
     September 2018.

83   Justin Levitt, "Who Draws the Lines? All about Redistricting," *Loyola Law
     School*, http://redistricting.lls.edu/who-partyfed20.php.

84   Maggie Astor and K.K. Rebecca Lai, "What's Stronger than a Blue Wave?
     Gerrymandered Districts," *New York Times*, 29 November 2018.

85   Michael Wines, "Will the Supreme Court End Gerrymandering? Arguments
     Begin This Week," *New York Times*, 25 March 2019.

86   German Lopez, "The Supreme Court's Big Racial Gerrymandering Decision,
     Explained," *Vox*, 22 May 2017.

87   Jessica Clarke, "Pennsylvania Supreme Court Strikes Down Gerrymandered
     Map That Hurt Black Voters," American Bar Association, 19 March 2018,
     https://www.americanbar.org/groups/litigation/committees/civil-rights/
     practice/2018/pennsylvania-supreme-court-strikes-down-gerrymandered-map-
     that-hurt-black-voters/.

88   Brennan Center for Justice, "League of Women Voters of Pennsylvania v.
     Commonwealth of Pennsylvania," 26 March 2018, https://www.brennancenter.
     org/our-work/court-cases/league-women-voters-pennsylvania-v-commonwealth-
     pennsylvania.

89   Clarke, "Pennsylvania Supreme Court."

Chapter Three

ENVIRONMENTAL (UN)PROTECTION

ON 3 APRIL 1968, THE DAY BEFORE HIS ASSASSINATION, the Reverend Martin Luther King Jr. reflected on the historical significance of the civil rights movement before a crowd of predominately African-American sanitation workers on strike in Memphis, Tennessee. "I'm just happy that God has allowed me to live in this period, to see what is unfolding," he said. "And I'm happy that He's allowed me to be in Memphis."[1] The city in which he was murdered was approaching civil war: civil on the part of the striking workers and supporting demonstrators, and war on the part of the city mayor and his police force, who repeatedly attacked the peaceful protestors with clubs, mace, and tear gas. That people on strike for fair pay and safe working conditions could be met with such violence was a shocking reminder of the latent power of white supremacy in America. It showed the lengths so many white Americans would go to in order to maintain the most fundamental of advantages over black Americans: not only would they deny them equal pay, but they would also actively suppress their request for the right for safe working conditions.

The protests themselves, a national news phenomenon, transformed the face of the civil rights movement, making otherwise hidden connections between environmental injustice and race embarrassingly obvious. It became clear that Memphis sanitation workers had been subjected to violence in subtler forms for years before the police force's brutal response to the protests—and in ways that shortened their lives, made them sick, affected the development of their children, and refused them a wage that would cover medical treatment for ailments related to their exposure to hazardous waste.

Environmental justice has been, and continues to be, a key component of the civil rights movement. Despite an increased awareness of environmental injustice among white Americans during the civil rights era, it would be more than 20 years before the federal government considered legislation to protect marginalized communities from disproportionate exposure to hazardous waste.

Change at the level of government policy would depend, ironically, on careful cooperation between residents and other, non-government groups, including scientists, religious communities, and academics— and would be met with consistent resistance from elected officials practicing bad-faith politics.

This chapter highlights a few key moments in the recent environmental justice movement to illuminate how bad-faith politics exploits racial and class divisions to perpetuate what I call environmental (un)protection. It argues that environmental injustice in the United States is the product of decades of bad-faith politics, originating in intentional policy decisions that reflect an unethical disregard for black lives. Similar to other civil rights violations, a denial of culpability and a stubborn resistance to reform characterize elected officials' actions. I frame the government's inaction on issues of environmental justice as a systemic form of racism that frames black life as waste and relies on ignorance, misinformation, and apathy to maintain its insidious power. The examples provided later in this chapter, each of which tells a story of grassroots activism in support of environmental justice for marginalized communities, demonstrate the political efficacy of interdisciplinary as well as interagency action and prompt pressing questions about the effectiveness of the electoral system in bringing about lasting change.

Decades of government inaction followed the Memphis sanitation workers' strike in 1968. It was not until 1994, more than a quarter-century later, that President Clinton took executive action to address environmental concerns pertaining explicitly to race, when he issued the memorandum "Federal Actions to Address Environmental Justice in Minority Populations and Low-Income Populations."[2] This sweeping memo set ethical parameters for all government agencies—not just those related to environmental protection—with regard to discrimination, ensuring that "all programs or activities receiving Federal financial assistance that affect human health or the environment do not directly, or through contractual or other arrangements, use criteria, methods, or practices that discriminate on the basis of race, color, or national origin."[3] Clinton's ambitious gesture toward environmental justice reform was quietly undermined by his successor, George W. Bush, who rolled back many of Clinton's policies and ensured that others received limited funding from Congress.

The federal government's failure to ensure adequate protections for marginalized communities is not a new phenomenon; it is a repeating pattern that cannot be solved with a simple change of administration. Trump's recent gutting of the Environmental Protection Agency demonstrates just how quickly progress can be undone. Trump's inhumane policy decisions may have been louder and starker than those of the last Republican president, but they reflect the same pattern of actively undoing the progress of the previous administration toward real equality.

It is perhaps no surprise, then, that political responses to the environmental justice movement have been lackluster at best. The political gains brought about by sustained attention to environmental issues equates to a slow-burning progress, the success of which may take generations to become apparent. In the meantime, newly elected officials have the power to cancel out the work of previous administrations with relative ease, meaning there are fewer political incentives for meaningful environmental justice reform policy. Moreover, the effects of mistreatment by politicians acting in bad faith often take generations to become discernible, and even then, it is difficult, albeit not impossible, to link health concerns among specific populations to the decisions of any single perpetrator. Since proving such connections takes considerable time, it is all too easy for elected officials to get away with cutting corners in public spending and putting the lives of marginalized people at risk to enrich themselves and make political gains. Thus the deliberate neglect of minority health concerns becomes evident only in hindsight, and the electoral system continues to benefit those who are best placed to take advantage of it.

Yet Trump's presidency may turn out to be the breaking point in this cycle of reforms and rollbacks—and not because political reform is more likely during this administration. To the contrary, this president's complete disregard for issues of racial justice is starker than that of his predecessors and is likely to negatively affect poor people of color for generations to come. Such can be seen in the essential elimination of the 2017 budget for the EPA's Office of Environmental Justice, which prompted the resignation in protest by its head, Mustafa Ali. In his resignation he stated, "Communities of color, low-income communities and indigenous populations are still struggling to receive equal protection under the law. These communities both rural and urban often live in areas with toxic levels of air pollution, crumbling or non-existent water and sewer infrastructure, lead in the drinking water ... and other hazardous waste sites."[4]

But where previous Republican presidents have sought to conceal the racist ideology that underpins their party's platform (which almost always includes spending cuts in health care and education that disproportionately affect people of color), Trump employs rhetoric that makes the motivation behind his policy decisions as clear as day. His illegal and inhumane border detention policy, which involves separating children from their parents, and his ban on Muslims entering the country are evils harder to mask than cutting costs by exposing vast swaths of the national population to hazardous chemicals. This is not only a story about Trump, however. It is the story of the advent of egregious bad-faith politics that emboldens the opponents of environmental justice to use any and all weapons of partisanship and marginalization to act against politics that would increase environmental justice. Bad-faith politics, including gerrymandering, voter suppression, and demagoguery, make it easier for environmentally unjust policies to be perpetuated, even against the wishes of the majority of citizens. Partisan actors will blatantly frame environmental issues as a zero-sum competition between corporate profit and meddlesome, profit-reducing environmental laws such as the *Endangered Species Act*.

In a sense, however, the boldness of Trump's racism makes it easier to fight against. His bigotry is so blatantly one of his core political motivations that it has engendered considerable political resistance from sectors outside of government, as well as unprecedented public awareness of how racial and environmental justice concerns in the United States are mutually imbricated and equally pressing. "Public awareness" may not have quite the same ring as "political action," but it may be more significant in the long term because it suggests that the tide of public opinion is beginning to turn, and thus that the American people are willing to hold politicians, whether in local, state, or federal government, accountable for acting in bad faith. There is more at stake now than before, and we have a heightened sense of those stakes. We have begun, for example, to ask whose job it is to ensure that the public has the information it needs to make informed decisions. Thousands of scientists, appalled at the new administration's antithetical approach to climate change and more aware than ever of the ethical breach that has occurred between the government and the public in the spread of misinformation surrounding this issue, have begun to act in accordance with a new ethics of responsibility to the public. The March for Science, a putatively nonpartisan event first held on Earth Day 2017, speaks to the questions facing scientists in the twenty-first century: Should they be required to adopt a nonpartisan politics even when their findings are misrepresented to the American people? What is the point in funding research if it has no real impact on policy and practice?

That scientists are self-identifying—many for the first time—as having a political stance (even if it is articulated, in nonpartisan terms, as "pro-science") is crucial to correcting the systemic problems underlying the environmental injustice movement, though this may be merely a happy coincidence, and not the primary motivation of pro-science activists. This kind of action may well bring with it the kind of awareness that necessitates broad ethics reform concerning the government's use or misuse of scientific fact, but it is unlikely to directly improve the living and working conditions of those disproportionately subjected to environmental hazards. In many respects, scientists are often too far removed from the lived condition, and the voices of those living these circumstances tend to be marginalized. As Jason Corburn observes, environmental justice discussions "systematically excluded local, non-expert knowledge by creating hard boundaries between scientific analysis and political values and between expert and lay judgments."[5] The vastly disparate experiences of these two groups—on the one hand, the victims of environmental abuse by government, and on the other hand, those who are qualified to recognize environmental abuse and empowered to call it out—means scientists concerned about the ethics of information gathering and sharing may not necessarily feel compelled to take partisan action to address the health concerns of minority populations. This incidental and largely symbolic promise of change, conceived and articulated from the perspective of a predominately white, male population of scientists who regularly express understandable hesitancy about the dangers of being labeled "political," lacks focus and intentionality. It does not specifically address the populations most affected by Trump's gutting of the EPA because its chief concern is the misrepresentation of facts, rather than injustice toward a particular population.

The history of the environmental justice movement teaches us that change in public policy is most effective when it develops out of the experience of victims. This is especially hard to achieve because the problem is difficult to discern and hard to prove. It requires dedicated funding to conduct the preliminary research to produce evidence of environmental abuses by government, and this financial support rarely comes from unreliable government initiatives. Indeed, Clinton's memorandum, which helped establish environmental justice reform as part of the Democratic party platform, was heavily informed by a report funded by the United Church of Christ (UCC) in 1987, titled "Toxic Wastes and Race." This report focused on inequality specifically in terms of environmental justice, using clear statistical evidence to make clear that race is the most discriminated variable in policy decisions related to public health: "Although socio-economic status appeared to play an important role in the location of commercial hazardous waste facilities, race still proved to be more significant. This remained true after the study controlled for urbanization and regional differences. Incomes and home values were substantially lower when communities with commercial facilities were compared to communities in the surrounding counties without facilities."[6] The study uses

deductive reasoning to conclude that the correlation between race
and exposure to toxic waste is the consequence of a deliberate abuse
of power; that government administrations at the local, state, and
federal level have for decades knowingly subjected communities of
color to hazardous living conditions. The authors frame this systemic
violence in the context of legislation designed to restrict local resistance to environmental injustice:

> Racial and ethnic communities have been and continue to be beset
> by poverty, unemployment and problems related to poor housing,
> education and health. These communities cannot afford the luxury
> of being primarily concerned about the quality of their environment
> when confronted by a plethora of pressing problems related to their
> day-to-day survival. Within this context, racial and ethnic communi-
> ties become particularly vulnerable to those who advocate the siting of
> a hazardous waste facility as an avenue for employment and economic
> development. Thus, proposals that economic incentives be offered to
> mitigate local opposition to the establishment of new hazardous waste
> facilities raise disturbing social policy questions.[7]

These proposals, designed to dissuade residents from legal action,
are a clear reminder of the boldness with which anti-Black racists
wield their privilege when threatened by organized dissent. The
UCC's report effectively proved that the city's aggressive response to
the Memphis sanitation workers' protest was not an isolated incident
but that it might be considered part of a more expansive pattern of
discrimination marked by indirect forms of violence toward marginalized communities. This was hard to prove, and harder still to use as
evidence with which to compel Congress to commit to reform.

Unfortunately, like gerrymandering and voter suppression, environmental racism is a form of discrimination that politicians can
currently wield without consequence, primarily because the public is
largely oblivious to the scope of this form of oppression. This is the
insidious nature of bad-faith politics; it is masked, and it is sometimes
difficult to discern by a public that has limited time and resources to
devote to civic affairs. The report published by the UCC in 1987 identifies environmental racism as evidence of an insidious, unwritten
social policy that actively targets those least prepared to organize or

protest in response. Given that victims are unlikely to even be aware that their ill health is the product of deliberate government policy, and given that funding is usually required to finance the scientific and statistical evidence needed to prove this connection, it is all the more surprising when residents *do* find ways of holding their representatives accountable for their abuse of power.

But even coordinated and politically organized voices beating the door down of their legislators often prove inadequate. There is a public-relations side of these maladies from the corporations' side. Philosopher Nancy McHugh puts it this way: "in many cases it is not their political representatives that they get traction from. Instead, they put so much pressure on corporations that it is easier for them to pull out than to continue the barrage of negative publicity."[8] As I will demonstrate using the examples that follow, meaningful and sustainable environmental justice reform depends on the production and dissemination of data and analysis that proves the pervasive existence of environmental-racial discrimination across the United States. The EPA's own definition of an environmental justice community requires scientific analysis to prove "a disproportionate impact from one or more environmental hazards" in order to earn the designation.[9] Thus it depends also on a clearly politicized research methodology— it requires a form of knowledge production that not only identifies the presence of toxic waste in the environment but also presupposes, records, and interprets the presence of this waste as a systemic and illegal form of discrimination. This kind of research demands that considerable resources for scientific and sociological research be redirected toward residents in geographic areas most in need and tailored to accommodate their specific needs as research subjects. The remainder of this chapter draws on Nancy McHugh's use of "situated knowledge"[10]—the idea that research data should arise from "collective experiences, not isolated knowers"[11]—to demonstrate that the issue of hazardous waste siting policy in the United States should be widely understood as a crisis of racism as much as it is already considered a crisis of public health. When Mustafa Ali resigned as head of the EPA's Office of Environmental Justice, he wrote, "When we listen and then work collaboratively with our stakeholders, some very productive actions can happen that have real positive change in local communities."[12] The recent water crisis in Flint, Michigan, is a good example of what happens when the knowledge produced by researchers does not define *environmental* justice as a matter of *racial* justice. It raises further questions about whether science alone provides the best vocabulary for articulating the problem: that environmental justice is already politicized, and that failing to recognize it not only misses the point but also makes the research itself unlikely to bring about any kind of successful and sustainable reform.

The lead poisoning disaster in Flint, Michigan, a predominantly black city, gained international news coverage back in 2016. Media outlets accurately presented it as a tragic and unintended consequence of a cost-cutting policy decision by local government. Their approach to the story also suggested that it was something of an isolated incident, which was not so accurate. Of children tested in 2014, 7 per cent in Flint tested positive for elevated levels of lead, compared to an astonishing 14 per cent in Cleveland, Ohio. According to a study published by the *New York Times* in 2016, across the nation, four million families with children are still exposed to dangerous levels of lead contained in household paint. Half a million of these make up 23.1 per cent of children living in Atlantic City, Philadelphia, and Allentown, Pennsylvania, the three cities affected most, all of them presenting with enough lead in their blood to "merit a doctor's attention." Writing for the *Times*, Michael Wines observed that the problem disproportionately affected poor neighborhoods, which are predominantly African American and Latino, and implied that the reason was unintentional neglect: the lead threat, he concluded, was "confined largely to poor neighborhoods with scant political clout," and there is "little official urgency—and increasingly, little money—to address it."[13] Yet even when it is widely known that the issue is cheaper to fix than to leave alone, public spending remains almost non-existent: according to a report published by a federal task force established in 2000, it would cost only $2.1 billion over 10 years to remove lead hazards from at-risk homes.

In Ohio, the state legislature set up a Lead Poisoning Prevention Fund in 2003 to support medical testing for children without insurance and to tackle the lead poisoning problem in older homes, but failed to give it any funding. This kind of neglect is an abuse of power that government agencies can get away with because they are not held responsible for their inaction, especially when it disproportionately affects people of color. Cleveland activist and director of the Northeast Ohio Black Health Coalition (NEOBHC) Yvonka Hall puts it this way: "the NEOBHC has been a leader in pushing for a lead safe Cleveland because of what lead does to our babies. We have children who are learning how to crawl on the floor of homes where there are environmental toxins coming through their windows, peeling paint, porches in need of repair in both low-income and rental property."[14] Clearly we understand what both Jesus and the rapper Tupac both understood, namely that our basic responsibility is ensuring that children are properly taken care of. Ms. Hall further implicates local and state government when she claims, "knowing what lead does to them developmentally, these babies are targeted because they are poor. The response back to families of children that are poisoned by lead to us has always been 'black people need to stop their children from eating lead.'"[15]

So what made Flint a special case? It is possible that Flint gained extensive media attention because, unlike most environmental disasters, the reason it happened in the first place was relatively easy to pinpoint. Flint residents began complaining about the quality of their water when the city switched its water source from Lake Michigan to the less costly Flint River. The city and the state both denied any change to the water quality until researchers at Virginia Tech University discovered high lead levels in the water and in children's blood. The crisis lent itself to a clear and coherent narrative in which no one could really be called a villain: unintentional neglect and poor decision making by thrifty government administrators led to a public health crisis, which the city denied because it feared legal action. Yet though this narrative made a name for Flint, it failed to result in any changes to government policy, and, three years later, it remains to be seen whether the crisis is actually over. Marc Edwards, the scientist responsible for discovering the elevated lead levels in Flint's drinking water, has been embroiled in a tedious series of lawsuits with ex-colleagues and local residents over the validity of his claims that the area's water now meets government standards. Scientists who previously supported Edwards's research are now calling into question his conclusions, the technicalities of which are too complex to sustain the interest of the American public for any longer.[16]

The crisis, it seems, has suffered from a problem of representation, and although the living conditions in Flint may be slowly improving, the disaster was never the catalyst for environmental justice that it could have been. While it was a documentary by Michael Moore, *Roger and Me* (1989), that highlighted Flint as a community in crisis, Flint occupied the public's political imagination as an incident of *racial* injustice because it was framed that way by a president who identified personally with the residents of Flint. On 4 May 2016, Obama spoke to the local community, using the disaster as a means to re-establish public trust in the state and thus to envision a better model of relationship between the government and the people. Advocacy by the first black president on behalf of an African-American population who felt they were not being heard helped elevate the issue to the level of public consciousness. As a representative of both big government and black experience, Obama was in a key position to bridge the gap between awareness and action on environmental racism. Using his platform, he presented the disaster in Flint as an opportunity to address environmental racism as a failure of the social contract: "And this kind of thinking—this myth that government is always the enemy; that forgets that our government is us—it's us; that it's an extension of us, ourselves—that attitude is as corrosive to our democracy as the stuff that resulted in lead in your water."[17]

A common example of what cracking and flaking lead paint looks like on a porch.

The relationship between the individual and the state is characterized by suspicion, Obama suggests, because politicians have not kept their promises to advocate for the lives of minorities. This "systematic neglect," he claimed, leads to "a lot of hidden disasters that you don't always read about and aren't as flashy, but that over time diminish the life of a community and make it harder for our young people to succeed. [...] Sometimes it takes a crisis for everybody to focus their attention. [...] There are a lot of small, quiet crises going on in the lives of people around this country. And this helps lift it up."[18] Though Obama's claim is that an individual crisis makes injustice visible where it once was not, it is arguable that his personal advocacy for victims—his framing of the disaster as an example of systemic racism and his awareness of the "quiet crises" faced by people of color that are considered less newsworthy but are no less heinous—helped "lift it up" more than the crisis itself, and, indeed, perhaps even more than the research carried out by Virginia Tech University, which focused on health care, rather than environmental justice, as a form of racism. The president's speech demonstrated the importance of perspective by grounding the disaster in terms of the lived experiences of poor minority families. His own early life, which shares some similarities with children in Flint, becomes, in this sense, an approach to research that takes into account the often unacknowledged contexts of individuals and groups, regardless of whether these contexts are racial, socioeconomic, or psychological. This raises the question: how much more could be achieved using the shared experiences of actual Flint victims, as well as those living in similar conditions?

One of the first environmental justice protests took place in 1982 in Warren County, North Carolina. The state of North Carolina chose to situate a hazardous waste landfill in Warren County. The landfill contained 30,000 cubic yards of soil contaminated with polychlorinated biphenyl. The residents of Warren County, primarily rural, poor, and African American, protested the landfill. Even with the support of national civil rights and environmental groups, the protests were unsuccessful and the landfill was constructed as planned.[19] However, while the group was not successful in stopping the landfill construction, their protest did contribute to the 1983 US General Accounting Office study that found that three out of four hazardous waste landfills in Region 4 (made up of eight Southern

states) were located in predominantly African-American communities, even though African Americans accounted for only 20 per cent
of the region's overall population.[20] According to Eileen McGurty,
a professor of environmental studies at Johns Hopkins University,
the Warren County protest helped to define environmental justice
as about more than just the physical impact: "The environmental
identity from Warren County, with its innovative framing of environmental problems as manifestations of civil rights injustices, profoundly impacted the movement's engagement with these tensions."[21]

For philosopher Nancy McHugh, the solution to environmental injustice, as well as to other forms of systemic racism that rely
on public confusion, ignorance, and helplessness, is to harness the
collective experiences of minority populations as a form of research.
Reform is not about what we know, she suggests, but about what we
do with what we know. The Flint debacle offers a useful counterpoint
to this idea. Whereas the American public became aware of the crisis
in Flint through research carried out by a white, male scientist and
his team (all of whom were removed from the material conditions
that were making Flint's residents sick and thus focused wholly on
environmental concerns), McHugh advocates for redirecting research
funding toward those whose narrative has been obscured. Funding,
she demonstrates, inevitably creates a narrative around the collective
experiences of groups deemed worthy of study, which results in situated knowledge. She explains, "all knowledge is situated in the sense
that all knowledge is generated from a knower's particular location,
which consists of the complex unfolding resulting from one's social,
material, epistemological, gendered, lived bodily experience."[22] But
an awareness of *how* knowledge is situated is fundamental to understanding why certain perspectives may have been kept from public
awareness, dismissed as biased or overly political, or actively stifled.
Minority perspectives are often excluded unconsciously, when research
funding is appropriated for white, affluent neighborhoods affected by
environmental hazards, rather than for poorer communities. Yvonka
Hall of the NEOBHC agrees, "funding minority organizations, or in
my case an African-American organization that focuses on African
American Health, is not a top priority. We are willing to speak and
act on the current atrocities that impact the community; however,
the neglect and mistreatment of minority populations is often more

intentional."[23] As the UCC report from 1987 suggests, government entities and corporations have long benefited from rhetoric and initiatives that persuade populations not to speak out, take legal action, or organize in protest, making community action even less likely. Where knowledge does originate in minority populations ("situated knowledge"), however, there is a greater chance of broad and lasting reform. Ms. Hall laments, "we live by the Mary Bethune way of thinking, looking at money as the least of the barriers needed to change the community but making the desire to serve as our paramount focus."[24] Such a position cements why the NEOBHC and other examples of community based knowledge (and action) are best suited to make the most impact in their respective communities.

As an example of situated knowledge being used to promote a critical platform on which to initiate reform, McHugh turns to a public-health crisis in the 1980s and 1990s that affected the predominantly African-American population of Bayview Hunters Point (BVHP), California, where an increased rate of breast-cancer diagnoses was thought to be "linked to industrial air pollution, water pollution, municipal waste, and radiation from a local Naval shipyard."[25] Though a report published in 1995 revealed much higher rates of breast cancer than the national average, congressional funding was allocated to other affected communities with whiter populations. This was not news to women living in Hunters Point, who had attempted to prove the link between pollution and ill health in their community for over a decade—without much success. And yet, in 1994, the year before the report was published, local mothers founded the Bayview Hunters Point Mothers Environmental Health and Justice Committee, a "grassroots community group" designed to "mobilize, train, and empower community mothers in the fight for environmental health and justice."[26] The Committee began to see serious results from their collective activism in 2006, when the city closed the Pacific Gas and Electric Co. power plant across the street from Hunters Point. That it took over a decade signifies the magnitude of the problem, as well as the remarkable amount of combined willpower and strategizing required to bring about meaningful change in communities where it is actively resisted.

A more recent example of situated knowledge bringing about environmental policy reform occurred in Detroit in March 2019. Residents of a predominantly black neighborhood in Detroit have been protesting the operation of an incinerator in their neighborhood since its construction in 1986. The incinerator, operated by Detroit Renewable Power, burned waste from the surrounding counties and turned it into electricity. Kim Hunter, an activist with the organization Breathe Free Detroit, observed, "Most of the waste [came] from whiter, more affluent communities, placing the burden of disposal on a mostly African American, lower-income community—classic environmental racism"[27] Though the residents of this community had been protesting and fighting for over 30 years, it wasn't until students from Wayne State University began conducting studies on the air quality and the health of the neighborhood's residents that the issue gained any traction. They wrote letters detailing their findings to Detroit mayor Mike Duggan and Representative Rashida Talib in mid-March 2019. By the end of the month, the incinerator had ceased operations.[28] It is telling that the neighborhood voices went unheeded for decades until organizations like Breathe Free Detroit and university researchers decided to get involved in the cause.

Environmental justice breakthroughs like these emphasize the persuasiveness of collective experience and the efficacy of group action and resources. Without such a perspective, we would lack awareness of the problem in context: for example, how environmental and health concerns are often exacerbated by the adjacent difficulties of subjugated groups, such as social isolation, poor nutrition (often a consequence of living in a "food desert"), institutional racism, poor access to health care, and higher rates of domestic violence. Stacy Ann Harwood observes, "Residents of wealthy neighborhoods tend to have higher quality services, more options, and regular infrastructure maintenance than those in many inner-city neighborhoods."[29] At the other end of the spectrum, the perception by government officials that minority neighborhoods were dirty reinforced to waste-management companies that locating their waste repositories in these neighborhoods would go unprotested.[30] As observed in the UCC report, minority populations are confronted with so many overlapping issues on a daily basis that they are unlikely to have the time or resources to consider decades-long legal action to prosecute the ethical violations of a city or state. In *Methodology of the Oppressed*, Chela Sandoval suggests that those in power make implicit assumptions about how minority populations will respond to injustice: "[i]t has been assumed that the oppressed will behave without recourse to any *particular* method, or rather, that their behavior consists of whatever acts one must commit in order to survive, whether physically or psychically."[31] It is thus all the more remarkable when victims of environmental injustice, which is so difficult to identify, rise above despondency and despair—which their oppressors are counting on—and instead share experiences, resources, and responsibilities. McHugh's formulation of what the Bayview women actually achieved is especially useful for understanding the magnitude of the task: "Working to locate, articulate, and critique one's own subject position when one is oppressed and then critically engaging the world from this perspective to create change is an unexpected methodology for people who have been subjugated."[32] Such an approach is not just unexpected; it is also elaborate and counterintuitive. It is a particularly sophisticated mode of organizing and articulating individual experience. It relies upon a comprehensive perspective of the self and a means of identifying as part of a recognizable and legible group with shared values and concerns. The current example is in Cleveland, where the Northeast Ohio Black Health Coalition coalesces, unapologetically, around black lives. It requires, then, a mindset that has evolved beyond what the early-twentieth-century psychologist W.E.B. Du Bois called "double consciousness": the sense, peculiar to African Americans, of "always looking at oneself through the eyes of others, of measuring one's soul by the tape of a world that looks on in amused contempt and pity."[33] The women of Hunters Point were able to organize effectively as a community because together they have enough life experience to know that nothing will be done to help them—they must help themselves. They were strategic in their desire to reach out for collaboration. By substantially collaborating with Greenaction, the residents of BVHP realized that they needed to work with people with a different set of skills and resources than they had. In essence, envisioning and organizing toward an ethical end (clearly identified by the name of the committee) made up of smaller, more manageable goals, these women engaged in what Patricia Hill Collins calls "visionary pragmatism."[34] Rising above the helplessness that had been thrust upon them but for which they had always been blamed, they knew that to have any chance of success they must act in good faith: with a provable, unshakeable commitment to collectively agreed-upon principles.

The continuing work of such organizations across the United States is crucial to preserving the future of the communities they protect: without the research, activism, and legal support provided by groups like the Bayview Hunters Point Mothers Committee, the Northeast Ohio Black Health Coalition, and others, the unjust suffering of marginalized communities would remain invisible except to those responsible for making them sick. By identifying as a group with clear objectives and values, and by railing against the forces that seek to isolate them from one another, victims and their families are fighting for their survival against the odds, as well as paving the way for broad environmental reform from which we will all benefit. In the age of Trump and the gutting of the EPA, it is more likely than ever that subjugated populations exposed to hazardous waste will find common ground and take it upon themselves to bring about reform—yet it is by no means their responsibility to do so. They will also face greater resistance from policies introduced to shut them down and weaken their resolve—and this is where the rest of us can help. Though the current political moment is marked by a heightened awareness of what can be achieved through grassroots activism, it should not fall exclusively to communities of color to correct the injustices perpetrated against them. The practice of situating knowledge requires dedicated research funding for communities adversely affected by environmental hazards, and this means acknowledging, in the first place, that communities of color are disadvantaged by circumstance. This is a statistical fact; there is no question of politics or bias—there is only the question of deciding whose lives matter, and whose do not. Scientists who err on the side of caution and profess themselves "nonpartisan" risk contributing to the issue by isolating data from its context and missing the big picture: that advocating for a safer environment cannot simply mean advocating for science; it must also mean advocating for racial justice—even if it means appearing "political." In this climate, we must not discourage research that focuses on underrepresented populations, but rather we should embrace this work as vital information we have been missing. We must recognize that this administration's disregard for truth, integrity, and reason are secondary to its disregard for black lives, and we must do everything in our power to let those lives speak.

Notes

1   Martin Luther King Jr., "I've Been to the Mountaintop," 3 April 1968,
     americanrhetoric.com/speeches/mlkivebeentothemountaintop.htm.

2   "Presidential Memorandum on Executive Order for Federal Actions to
     Address Environmental Justice in Minority Populations and Low-Income
     Populations," *EPA*, www.gao.gov/assets/710/701401.pdf.

3   Ibid.

4   Mustafa Ali, Resignation Letter, Environmental Protection Agency, 8 March
     2017, thinkprogress.org/mustafa-ali-environmental-justice-epa-trump-
     3d4cf00f558a/.

5   Jason Corburn, "The Discourse of a Community-Based Cumulative Exposure
     Assessment," *Environmental Management* 29.4 (2002): 451.

6   Commission for Racial Justice: United Church of Christ, "Toxic Wastes and
     Race: A National Report on the Racial and Socio-Economic Characteristics of
     Communities with Hazardous Waste Sites," 1987, xiii, https://www.nrc.gov/
     docs/ML1310/ML13109A339.pdf.

7   Ibid, xi–xii.

8   Interview with Nancy McHugh, 24 July 2019.

9   Ryan Holifield, "Defining Environmental Justice and Environmental Racism,"
     Urban Geography 22.1 (2001): 78–90. McHugh stated in our interview that "this
     definition is more robust than this in terms of how it identifies a community as
     an environmental justice community. For example, rural white communities do
     not get that designation, but Black rural communities do. On a side note, there
     is a Turkish community in Dayton that is an EJ community and the site of an
     EPA Superfund site. One of the reasons it is interesting is most parents don't
     speak English and the children serve as translators between the parents and
     EPA."

10   The term was developed by Donna Haraway in 1990 in her article "Simians,
     Cyborgs and Women" and was picked up by numerous theorists. McHugh's
     unique contribution is her concept of "transactionally situated knowledge,"
     which expands upon Haraway's and others' development of situated knowledge.

11   Nancy McHugh, *The Limits of Knowledge: Generating Pragmatist Feminist Cases
     for Situated Knowing* (Albany: SUNY Press, 2015), 44.

12   Ali, Resignation Letter.

13   Michael Wines, "Flint Is in the News, but Lead Poisoning Is Even Worse in
     Cleveland," *New York Times*, 3 March 2016.

14   Interview with Yvonka Hall, 14 July 2019.

15 Ibid.

16 Sukanya Charuchandra, "Scientist Who Blew the Whistle on Flint Water Sues Activists," *Scientist*, 27 July 2018.

17 Barack Obama, in Katie Reilly, "Read President Obama's Speech in Flint on Water Crisis," *Time*, 5 May 2016.

18 Ibid.

19 Susan Cutter, "Race, Class and Environmental Justice," *Progress in Human Geography* 19.1 (1995): 111–22.

20 Robert D. Bullard, "Dismantling Environmental Racism in the USA," *Local Environment* 4.1 (1999): 5–19.

21 Eileen McGurty, *Transforming Environmentalism* (New Brunswick, NJ: Rutgers University Press, 2007), 112.

22 McHugh, *Limits of Knowledge*, 44.

23 Interview Yvonka Hall, 14 July 2019.

24 Ibid.

25 McHugh, *Limits of Knowledge*, 40.

26 Ibid., 43.

27 Kim Moore, "We Won: Environmental Activists Claim Victory after Detroit Incinerator Closes," *Energy News Network*, 9 July 2019.

28 O. Doubrovski, V. Holsey, M.I. Noor, D. Wilson, D. Jordan, and K. Campbell-Voytal, "Living in the Shadow of Detroit Renewable Power," Wayne State University, familymedicine.med.wayne.edu/research_day_2019/dfmphs_research_day_2019_program_-_final_revised.pdf.

29 S.A. Harwood, "Environmental Justice on the Streets: Advocacy Planning as a Tool to Contest Environmental Racism," *Journal of Planning Education and Research* 23 (2003): 25.

30 Carl A. Zimring, *Clean and White: A History of Environmental Racism in the United States* (New York: New York University Press, 2015), 145.

31 Chela Sandoval, *The Methodology of the Oppressed* (Minneapolis: University of Minnesota Press, 2000), 175.

32 McHugh, *Limits of Knowledge*, 40.

33 W.E.B. Du Bois, *The Souls of Black Folk: Essays and Sketches* (Chicago: A.C. McClurg & Co., 1904), 3.

34 Patricia Hill Collins, *Fighting Words: Black Women and the Search for Justice* (Minneapolis: University of Minnesota Press, 1998), 188.

Chapter Four

THE GREAT AMERICAN TEAR

America and the Gun

The stars
In your flag,
America,
Are like bullet holes.
—*Yevgeny Yevtushenko*

ON 6 SEPTEMBER 1949, HOWARD UNRUH WALKED OUT of the three-bedroom apartment he shared with his mother and began walking down a busy commercial street in Camden, New Jersey. A decorated marksman, Unruh had returned from the war with a very particular set of skills that simply didn't translate into civilian life. He felt alienated and underappreciated. He kept records in his diary of those who had offended him, fantasizing about "retaliation," which would, he said, come when the time was right.[1]

That time came on the morning of 6 September. Unruh rose, dressed himself smartly in a summer suit complete with polka-dot bow tie, and had his breakfast with his mother. After breakfast, he descended to the basement, where he had a makeshift shooting range and a cache of rifles, handguns, and ammunition. When he emerged from the apartment, he was holding a loaded Luger P09 in his hand. In his pockets were a second loaded clip, 16 loose cartridges, a tear-gas canister, and a six-inch knife. It was just after 9 a.m., and within a few short hours, newspaper hawkers all over the country would be shouting his name on street corners. A "quiet, well-dressed young man" had, said the *Leominster Daily Enterprise*, gone "on a maniacal shooting rampage," killing a dozen and injuring five in only 12 minutes.[2] It was Unruh's *Walk of Death*—America's first modern mass shooting.[3]

The first shot Unruh fired was at a passing bread delivery truck, narrowly missing the driver. His next shots came as he entered the shoe-repair shop, where he shot the cobbler twice, killing him. He walked from there to the barbershop. A six-year old boy sat in the chair having his hair cut. Unruh entered and, calling out the barber by name, shot him in the stomach. The barber tried to shield the boy from Unruh's fire, but the next shot caught the child in the chest. The barber collapsed on the floor before Unruh crossed the room and shot him point blank in the head. The boy's mother, ignored by Unruh, picked up her boy and clutching him to her chest, ran shrieking out of the barbershop—the boy would die before reaching the hospital.

He moved from the barbershop toward his primary target, the drug store and its proprietors, the Cohens, shooting randomly through the locked doors of the tavern on the way. At the entrance to the drug store, he shot and killed a man who, according to Unruh, didn't get out of his way fast enough. Inside were the Unruhs' neighbors, the Cohens. The couple had been a thorn in Unruh's side since he had returned from the war. They argued frequently—most often about Howard's use of the Cohens' gate, which he would use to cut through their yard. Unruh had installed a gate of his own and, on the morning of 5 September (the morning before his Walk of Death), he rose to find his new gate destroyed. He was convinced that this was the work of the Cohens—the proverbial last straw.

The Cohens, who had heard the shooting, were hiding in the adjoining apartment. Unruh first found Rose Cohen in the closet.

He shot her multiple times through the closet door before opening the door and shooting her in the face. He then found her husband, Maurice Cohen, on the roof. Unruh shot him in the back, and the chemist's lifeless body fell into the street. Finally, he found Mrs. Cohen's 63-year-old mother, who was on the phone with the police. He shot her multiple times before he left the house, leaving only one survivor: the Cohens' 12-year-old son, whom Rose Cohen had pushed into a closet just moments before Unruh had discovered her hiding in a closet of her own.

On the street in front of the drug store, Unruh began to fire randomly at motorists. He leaned into the open window of a car that had slowed down and shot the driver, killing him. Re-emerging from the window, he fired at a car that had stopped at a red light, killing a woman and her mother and fatally injuring her nine-year-old son (he would die 18 hours later on the operating table, becoming Unruh's thirteenth victim). Unruh looked up to see a curtain moving in a window across the street, and he fired at what he thought might be somebody about to return fire. His shots killed an infant playing in the curtains.

Unruh entered the tailor's shop, where he found the proprietor's wife. Through the open door, witnesses could hear the tailor's wife pleading with Unruh to spare her. Without a word, he shot her at close range, killing her instantly. From there, he walked toward his home, stopping briefly at the home of a neighbor, where he fired his last two shots at a couple as he burst into their home, injuring them both, but not killing either of them. He then barricaded himself in his mother's apartment. Police surrounded the building and, after a volley of tear gas, brought him out in cuffs. His Walk of Death was over. As the police drove him back to the station, Unruh sat in cuffs and, calmly, confessed to everything. He would have killed 1,000, he said, if he had had enough bullets.

When Unruh was evaluated by psychologists, he displayed most of the hallmarks we've learned to associate with mass shooters. He was an alienated white male, a ticking time bomb of impotence and rage. World War II had given Unruh an opportunity to practice killing humans, and he took an inordinate amount of pleasure in his wartime killing work. He may have concealed this from his comrades, but he kept a diary, each page filled with records of his kills on the battlefield. He marked the day, hour, and place of each German he killed, describing the corpses in grisly, meticulous detail.

When he returned from the European theater, he kept up this habit of writing in his diary. He believed that his neighbors talked about him behind his back (he may have been right, for he undoubtedly cut a strange figure in the neighborhood, and the open secret of his homosexuality marked him as a deviant at a time when homosexuality was still illegal). He made cryptic notations in his diary, writing "Ret. W.T.S." (Retaliate When Time Suitable) and "D.N.D.R." (Do Not Delay Retaliation) next to his neighbors' names.

* * *

Unknowingly, when Unruh exited his apartment, his Luger hanging slackly at his side, he was introducing a new kind of toxin into America's bloodstream. We were a gun-obsessed nation long before Unruh's Walk of Death, but we hadn't yet crossed that threshold— hadn't yet had our eyes opened to the kind of carnage one determined man could produce if armed with twentieth-century firepower and a pocketful of ammunition. Unruh exploded our notions of what was possible. He lifted the bar for the killers who came after him. He lived (confined in a mental institution) until 2009—long enough to see the kind of killing spree he inaugurated become woefully commonplace, long enough to see mass shooters like himself become vivid and recurring features of modern American life, long enough even to see the Columbine killers push America into its new and grisly age of the rampage killer.

In all these long years bridging Unruh's Walk of Death and today, we *could* have done something to address the true roots of the problem: the combination of our national obsession with the gun as a symbol of unlimited personal freedom and the widespread availability of guns. We could have adopted (at any point, really) sensible gun control,[4] but we have not done so. As a nation, we have sat on our hands because we are enthralled with the gun and with all that it evokes (freedom, masculine power, and personal protection). Because we accept these connections reflexively, we have allowed bad-faith arguments to turn our heads, allowing the NRA and its talking heads to turn each new tragedy into yet another opportunity for gun manufacturers to push more and deadlier weapons into American consumers' hands. The personal firearm is, we have decided, quintessentially American, and any attempt to regulate the manufacture or the purchase of firearms is therefore un-American to its core. This is the bad-faith argument we have allowed to frame the gun debate, and, quite literally, it's killing us.

A student protesting during National Walkout Day at the Capitol, Washington, DC, 14 March 2018.

The problem, or at least our difficulty in addressing it, is nearly as old as this country. It began when the smoke was still clearing from the Revolutionary War, in the final decade of the eighteenth century. James Madison offered a series of corrective proposals that would address what anti-federalists saw as deficiencies in the Constitution. There were 12 of these proposals when Madison drafted them, but only 10 of them were added to the constitution—10 amendments, including the second:

> A well regulated Militia, being necessary to the security of a free State, the right of the people to keep and bear Arms, shall not be infringed.

For nearly a century and a half, it was quite literally the wild, wild west out there, with no federal regulations[5] concerning the sale or ownership of firearms. It wasn't until automatic weapons began appearing with increasing frequency on America's streets that the call for national gun-control legislation was answered. The *National Firearms Act* (*NFA*) of 1934 and the *Federal Firearms Act* (*FFA*) of 1938 were Roosevelt's responses to the increasing number of automatic weapons being used in the commission of crimes. The St. Valentine's Day Massacre (the Capone-orchestrated gangland slaying that resulted in seven deaths), Bonnie and Clyde's spree of mayhem, and Dillinger's string of bank robberies (10 of them in 1933) demanded nothing less than a national response. The *NFA* created a $200 tax[6] on certain kinds of guns that were popular among the criminal classes (machine guns and short-barreled rifles and shotguns), and the *FFA* forced those who sold guns to keep detailed records of these sales. Gun owners also had to register their firearms with the Secretary of the Treasury.

Of course, there were challenges to these laws, but the Supreme Court chose to interpret the Second Amendment narrowly, rebuffing plaintiffs who wanted to use the Constitution as a shield. In the 1939 case *United States v. Miller*,[7] for instance, the court could find no evidence that a sawed-off shotgun "had some reasonable relationship to the preservation or efficiency of a well regulated militia"; they ruled that the Second Amendment did *not* guarantee "the right to keep and bear such an instrument."[8] The justices saw no reason to question the continued relevance of the Second Amendment, but they did show a willingness to place some limits on its interpretation.

It wasn't until the 1960s were drawing to their close that the gun-control debate widened to include questions about not just what kind of guns Americans could own but also what kind of Americans should be allowed access to firearms at all. Americans were beginning to question the belief—perhaps appropriate when the country was still young, but growing less so as the wild frontier disappeared and the federal government became less provisional—that the gun and the American male needed each other to be truly complete. The gun had become woven into America's mythology, and it took a trio of high-profile assassinations (JFK, MLK, and RFK) and another mass shooting (this one from a clock tower in Austin, Texas) for us to step back and wonder out loud whether it was time to bring to a close America's long-toothed age of the gun.

Even then, journalists with both feet in the mainstream were criticizing the United States for its fetishization of firearms. *Time*, only two weeks after the assassination of Robert F. Kennedy, published a cover story on guns in America, enlisting Roy Lichtenstein for the cover. Lichtenstein's image is so striking because the viewer stares down the barrel of the gun. The man who holds the gun is not pictured. The artist had to place the wrist at an almost impossible angle to remove the shooter from the frame, but that's exactly what he's done, and the intention is clear. *Time* had featured both Lee Harvey Oswald and his widow on its cover in the aftermath of the JFK shooting, reflecting America's obsession at the time with the assassin. Five years later, following two more high-profile assassinations, the editors of *Time* wanted to change the focus, shifting America's attention from the shooter to his weapon. What is clear from the image on the cover is that what will be under discussion here is the tool—the instrument of death, not the grim musician who plays it.[9]

After a brief preamble, the story begins with these words:

> All too widely, the country is regarded as a blood-drenched, continent-wide shooting range where toddlers blast off with real rifles, housewives pack pearl-handled revolvers, and political assassins stalk their victims at will.
>
> The image, of course, is wildly overblown, but America's own mythmakers are largely to blame. In U.S. folklore, nothing has been more romanticized than guns and the larger-than-life men who wielded them. From the nation's beginnings, in fact and fiction, the gun has been provider and protector.[10]

Americans were at least starting to question whether guns were indeed the protective force their manufacturers claimed them to be. Following the first Kennedy assignation, the public had called on the government to ban mail-order sales of firearms (Lee Harvey Oswald had purchased the gun that killed Kennedy by responding to an ad in *American Rifleman*), but the federal government had dragged its feet, with bills stalling in the House. With the Robert Kennedy assassination, though, the public outcry became more intense and more difficult for lawmakers to ignore. Within two weeks, the House passed the *Gun Control Act* (*GCA*). Three months later, on 22 October, President Lyndon Johnson signed the act into law. The *GCA* banned mail-order firearm purchases, demanded that gun merchants keep records of gun sales, and banned felons, "mental incompetents," and minors from purchasing guns. It also limited the kind of guns that could be imported into the United States, allowing only for the import of guns that had a clear "sporting purpose."

Even the NRA's president at the time said that these new restrictions were reasonable. The NRA successfully lobbied against universal registration and mandatory licensing, calling these measures "unduly restrictive," but they were on board with the rest.[11] The organization, which started in 1871 as a marksmanship club, had always stood firmly on the side of gun owners, but it had not been against *all* forms of gun-control legislation. It had actually helped shape some of America's earliest attempts at gun control, and in the 1960s the NRA backed gun-control measures—first, California introduced as a bill to outlaw open carry (then practiced defiantly by members of the nascent Black Panthers), and then, a year later, national gun-control legislation restricting gun ownership and inter-state commerce. Pictures of armed black men occupying California's State Capitol and stories of the Black Panthers' "police patrols," which saw armed black men ensuring that young black men knew their rights and that police respected these rights, were enough to convince NRA leadership that *some* forms of gun control were necessary.

Less than a decade later, though, the NRA had changed tack. The organization's initial support for gun control had been seen as a way to keep guns out of the hands of undesirables (i.e., black males). In the 1970s, though, a growing faction of NRA hardliners framed the issue differently, presenting gun control (*any* gun control) as something of a slippery slope. If the federal government could keep guns out of black hands, what would prevent them from similarly restricting white "law-abiding" gun owners?

This led to a changing of the guard in the NRA—a dramatic rightward shift that moved an already conservative-leaning organization into the hyper-partisan territory it has occupied ever since. Led by Harlon Carter, the New Right, a fusing of socially conservative factions of the Republican Party with the religious right, staged something of a putsch at the NRA's annual meeting in Cincinnati, pushing out centrists in favor of rabid ideologues like Carter who promised to oppose all forms of gun control. Carter became the new face of the NRA, and his extreme positions became the new NRA dogma: guns in dangerous hands, he said, are "the price we pay for freedom."

Over the next eight years under Carter's leadership, the NRA would endorse its first political candidate (Ronald Reagan) and would triple in size, growing from one million members in 1977 to more than three million in 1985.[12] The NRA became the natural home of dog-whistle politics and its now-trademark single-issue inflexibility. It may have, at one time, been an organization with which compromise was possible, but that time ended quite suddenly when Harlon Carter and his New Right acolytes seized control of the organization.

Americans began digging in, with either side of the gun-control debate settling into trenches in decidedly partisan political territory. The NRA had, through its open alliance with the Republican Party, seized control of the gun-control debate and, with powerful messaging, had managed to convince a wide swath of Americans that guns were necessary to the exercise of personal freedom.

As the NRA was seizing complete control of the gun debate and foreclosing any possibility of a political response, the toxin that Unruh had introduced into America's bloodstream was seething beneath the surface, manifesting in visible symptoms every few years. In the 1980s, mass shootings began to appear more frequently, but crime was on the rise nearly everywhere, so we treated the problem as a subset of the larger problem of crime in America. But the crime wave crested in the early 1990s. Violent crime began to fall. Mass shootings, though, continued unabated and, as the decade drew to a close, we turned a corner. With Columbine, we entered a new age of American gun violence: the age of the rampage shooter.

Columbine seemed to be the moment when the toxin entered a new phase. The blood-borne illness went airborne, spreading more quickly than even the most pessimistic outlooks could have foreseen. There had, according to a *New York Times* piece immediately following Columbine, been 100 rampage killers between Unruh and Columbine, with the trend line curving slightly in the latter decades.[13] In the years following Columbine, though, the number of rampage killers began to climb. The toxin was spreading.

We understood that we were ill, but we couldn't (and still can't) agree on the roots of the issue or the course of treatment that should follow. In the media, everything received the blame—those on the right blamed violent video games, movies, and heavy-metal music (Marilyn Manson being a particular target for conservative finger-pointing); those on the left suggested that the boys had been targeted by bullies and this had left them with deep emotional scars that led them to do what they did. A narrative emerged of the bullied and ostracized teen taking revenge on those who made his daily high-school existence a torment—whether this reflected the actual facts (which it didn't) was unimportant. It was a way for Americans to make sense of the tragedies without any deep soul searching or close scrutiny of the deeper underlying causes.

The Columbine shooters didn't want to get even with bullies or to emulate their video-game avatars. They, like Unruh, wanted to amass a body count, with Dylan Klebold writing before the shooting began that he wanted to inflict "the most deaths in U.S. history." Armed with high-powered weapons of war, they got the infamy they were after, becoming, for a time, the deadliest high-school shooters in US history (they have since been supplanted by the Parkland shooter).

They set a grisly precedent. In the decade and a half following Columbine, school shootings and other rampage killings began appearing more regularly. A recent study commissioned by the FBI found that there were 160 active-shooter incidents between 2000 and 2013 (a little less than one per month), resulting in 486 deaths and 557 injuries (not including the shooter or shooters). If we zoom in a little closer, the trend line becomes more troubling. Between 2000 and 2006, there was an average of 6.4 incidents annually; between 2007 and 2013, this number nearly tripled, rising to 16.4 incidents annually.[14] In the years following the study, mass killings have continued to rise. There were 20 active shooters in 2014, 2015, and 2016, 30 of them in 2017, and 27 in 2018.

And, at the time of writing, 2019 looks as though it will be no different. Last night was 3 August. As I fell asleep, in an Illinois hotel room, talking heads on CNN were discussing a mass shooting at a Wal-Mart in El Paso, Texas. After publishing his manifesto online, a young white supremacist had taken 20 lives. When I woke up the next morning, 4 August, it was to news of a shooting in Dayton,

Ohio—only short miles from my home. I stepped outside my hotel room to try to clear my head, and my phone rang to inform me that one of the families I am close with had lost a child in the shooting. Not long after, I sat on the phone with the shocked and grieving parents and, together, we bowed our heads in prayer. I prayed fervently and earnestly, asking God to guide and help us in these dark times. I wonder if it will take some form of supernatural intercession for anything to change. I know that, this time next week, the nationwide outrage will have subsided and the now-age-old talking points will have won out once again. The needle will seem to move then find its center once again. We'll be no wiser and no more determined than before. We'll be as unwilling as ever to accept that our gun culture is the one feature that clearly distinguishes this country from all others. There are unacceptably high levels of gun violence in South and Central America and in Africa, but they don't have the same kind of problem we do with rampage shooters. A recent study that looked at 292 mass shootings globally found that 90 of them took place in America; though we have only 5 per cent of the world's population, we account for 31 per cent of its mass shootings.[15] What is it about America that makes us so prone to attacks of this nature, and why have they risen so sharply over the last two decades?

The obvious answer is availability—particularly the availability of high-powered urban-assault weapons that seem tailor-made for the kinds of mass shootings we've seen become more frequent over the past two decades. In 2001, in the midst of the assault-weapons ban, the firearms industry produced around 60,500 AR-15s (mostly in a watered-down version that complied with tight restrictions); 10 years later, untethered by legislation, they made 1.27 million of them.[16] The guns no longer merely looked like military issue; they now performed in nearly identical ways.

The NRA managed to convince gun owners that Obama would soon be coming for their guns, so collectors got while the getting was good, snatching them up in record numbers. They also leaned into messaging that explicitly connected assault rifles with freedom and patriotism, calling them "America's Rifle." The gun became a must-have item for all those who took this messaging to heart. The ultimate in-home defense, the AR-15 is the gun with the most stopping power, the gun that makes the loudest statement about your love of country, your willingness to defend your castle, your virility. What's more, in our hyper-partisan age, owning an AR-15 has become a political statement—a middle finger raised to liberals and their increasingly urgent calls for gun control. There are millions of these guns in America (estimates of how many assault rifles in America range from 8 to 15 million, and, with one in five guns sold in America being an assault rifle, that number is rising with each passing day).

The AR-15 is, undoubtedly, one of the loudest statements (political and otherwise) available to the American male (and particularly to the alienated white male, who, in his isolation and his rage, is, with alarming frequency, choosing to make that statement with bloody consequences). Those men who, filled with rage, take an AR-15 in their hands have at their disposal a gun like no other, a purpose-built killing machine of the highest order. An unmodified AR-15 can fire at about the same rate as a semi-automatic pistol, but the amount of force it puts into each bullet makes all the difference. Comparing a handgun to an AR-15 is like comparing an ice pick to a harpoon. "A handgun [wound]," says Dr. Peter Rhee, a trauma surgeon and retired Navy captain with more than 24 years of service, "is simply a stabbing with a bullet. It goes in like a nail"; because of its high-velocity firing power and the shape of the bullet, Rhee says, shooting somebody with an AR-15 is like shooting somebody "with a Coke can."[17] It quite literally blows a hole through the middle of whoever is unlucky enough to be in front of one.

This was the gun used by the shooters in yesterday's shooting in El Paso, and it was the one used in this morning's shooting three miles from where I write. It was the gun used by the shooters in Sandy Hook, Aurora, San Bernardino, Parkland, Newtown, Sutherland Springs, Orlando, and, of course, Las Vegas, where the shooter used a bump stock to turn his AR-15 into a de facto automatic rifle, which allowed him to take more than 50 lives and injure 10 times that many. Thanks to the yet-unclosed gun-show loophole, which allows private gun sales to take place without the purchaser having to show ID or pass a background check, it is virtually impossible to keep these guns out of the hands of motivated buyers.

Without question, the ubiquity of guns (and particularly guns like the AR-15 that have, at best, a questionable place in civil society) contributes significantly to America's unique problem with rampage killers. Legislation might address this issue, but, with each passing day, the size of the problem legislators are facing grows. Long ago, we crossed that tipping point when the problem of mass killings went from epidemic to endemic—the point of no return when an isolated illness ceases to be containable or even treatable without radical and universal treatment. Unless we change something soon, rampage killings will become a permanent feature in the American landscape, a scar carved across our land every bit as deep and lasting as the Grand Canyon.

We've sat by and watched as the NRA has tied together firearms and patriotism with a Gordian knot. Severing the knot with one swing of the pen may pull this country into open and perhaps bloody conflict with its most passionate gun owners. We let what might have been our moment to act decisively pass us by. We did *nothing* when 20 children between the ages of six and seven were gunned down by a young man with an assault rifle. If that wasn't enough to spur us to action, what kind of horror do we have to witness before we act? When does Harlon Carter's *price of freedom* become more than we are collectively willing to pay? If not Sandy Hook, if not Las Vegas, when?

We are outraged each time we hear the news of a mass shooting. We fume and fulminate, calling the shooters every name in the book. They are, we say, heartless monsters, deranged psychopaths, cold-blooded murderers, but this notoriety (a perverted form of celebrity status) is more alluring than we might realize. In the eight years after Columbine, school shooters modeled themselves on the killers, with two-thirds of school shooters citing Eric Harris and Dylan Klebold as inspiration for their crimes; researchers found that at least 17 attackers between 1999 and 2014 were inspired by the two, and a further 36 teenagers were foiled in their plans to do to their classmates and teachers what Eric and Dylan had done.[18] Sensationalized coverage of mass killings in America has given those with the stomach for mass murder an all-too-easy path to becoming a household name. On online message boards (particularly on sites like 8chan—a veritable hotbed for homegrown white-nationalist terrorists), young white males are dabbling in fringe extremism. The counterculture rebel has been replaced by more noxious forms of rebellion. The isolated and ostracized have found fellowship in some of the internet's darkest corners, and, from there, they fantasize gleefully about mass murder and revenge. For some, this is an act of play—a short-lived experimentation with the limits of the permissible. For others, though, the game becomes very real, the line between fantasy and reality blurring and then evaporating.

Each new shooting explodes the limits of the possible. With Sandy Hook, Orlando, Las Vegas, California, El Paso, and now my town, Dayton, the previously inconceivable became conceivable. The contagion gathers force and spreads further and further—aided by sensationalized media coverage. "'The transmission mechanism,' says Philip Cook, professor of public policy at Duke University, 'seems to be nothing more or less than that it's an idea that's in the air. So you have these kind of catastrophic consequences from what seems a minor change in the environment.'"[19] We react with attention and fascination, with social media and water cooler outrage, but not with action. Unknowingly, we are spreading the contagion, not fighting it.

Thanks to our inaction, we've watched in helpless paralysis as mass shootings have proliferated. We have not changed the climate in any measurable way. Quite the opposite. If anything, guns are even easier to obtain than they were in 1999, and the contagion of rampage killers has made landfall in nearly every state in the nation. We could have done something (after Columbine, after Sandy Hook, after Vegas, after El Paso and Dayton), but we've allowed the NRA to convince us that legislation won't work.

It has worked, though. When, after a spate of mass shootings in Australia, the government brushed aside conservative opposition and passed the National Firearms Agreement, the result was a complete elimination of mass shootings; they had 13 of them before 1996, when the NFA was passed (only 12 days after the Port Arthur Massacre), and none of them since.[20] In New Zealand, the response to the Christchurch shootings was the immediate introduction of a ban on semi-automatic, military-style weapons like the AR-15. New Zealand's legislators voted nearly unanimously (119 to 1), striking while the iron was hot and tempers were high. Here in America, though, we are told by gun-rights advocates that the aftermath of the most recent rampage killing is *not the time* to be talking about gun control. They pivot quickly to their established talking points, arguing for more guns rather than fewer as the solution to the issue. They are more interested in protecting our obscenely broadly interpreted Second Amendment than in doing *anything* to curb the epidemic.

The NRA and its corporate partners are actually motivated to do less than nothing about America's mass-shooting epidemic. For a time, gun-rights advocates found themselves on the defensive in the aftermath of shootings, but they've managed to turn mass shootings into yet another sales pitch. They no longer move gradually from the defensive to the offensive position; they forego defense entirely, calling immediately and urgently for *more* guns in public spaces and fretting about the imminent arms seizure that will target law-abiding gun owners. This toxic combination means that mass shootings are driving gun sales rather than gun regulations. This means that gun ownership responds in trackable ways to mass shooting events. Each time there is a shooting, and particularly when the weapon involved is, for example, an AR-15, sales shoot up in the days following the event, with buyers citing worry about a lack of future availability.

This is also true for gun accessories, like the bump stock. Only gun enthusiasts could have told you what a bump stock was on the morning of 1 October 2017, but the next day, after extensive reporting on the deadly efficacy of the bump stock used by the Las Vegas shooter, gun stores all over the country were fielding calls from collectors who wanted to get their hands on one before bans went into place.[21] Indeed, the Trump administration outlawed bump stocks a little more than a year after the Vegas shooting, giving owners 90 days to surrender their assault weapon mods to authorities. Even though owning a bump stock is now the equivalent of owning a machine gun (i.e., a felony), law-enforcement officials have reported that they have seen very few instances of owners surrendering the now-illegal devices, and because bump stocks do not come printed with a serial number, it is impossible to track the devices and the people who own them.[22] With each new tragedy, the problem of how to disarm Americans (or at least how to reduce civilian firepower to more reasonable levels) grows larger. Doing so after Columbine would have been a logistical nightmare—doing so now, following the more than decade-long surge in assault-weapon production and sales in the United States, would be, well, *better late than never.*

Trump offered thoughts and prayers when he addressed the nation following the Parkland shooting, a learned and impulsive response that has grown now unmoving. In his scripted remarks, he reminded the nation's children that they are not alone and that there are people who will do *anything* to help. Trump promised to tackle "the difficult issue of mental health,"[23] staying on NRA script by focusing on the mentally deranged killer, as though it was mental illness and mental illness alone that allowed him to take as many lives as he did. He urged them to seek the counsel or assistance of teachers, family members, police officers, or faith leaders—but not, apparently, their elected leaders, for they will do nothing to help. As unassailable as the problem seems to be, a handful of plucky high-school students have begun to show us a way forward, showing us an example of the kind of courage we will need even to approach (let alone tackle) this issue. These high-school students—survivors of the Parkland school shooting—have turned their status as victims into a powerful lobbying force. They've used social media as a rallying point rather than an echo chamber, pushing for (and getting) floods of phone calls to representatives and a million-strong march on Washington complete with stirring speeches from survivors and allies. Even if they haven't produced the dramatic changes that they have called for, they've moved the public needle. They've paid a cost. They have exposed themselves to the slings and arrows of outraged pundits and menacing trolls. The young activists have borne these threats and insults bravely, knowing that their status as survivors places them in the best position to turn the tide.

Those who oppose them, armed with bad-faith arguments about the efficacy of intervention, want to present the problem as though it were unsolvable—as though the only solution is to meet the threat of violence with yet-deadlier threats of violence. Gun-clutching Republicans (and no small number of purple-state Democrats) argue that nothing can be done: cities like Chicago and Los Angeles, they say, are already "gun-free zones," which proves, so they say, that gun control doesn't work. These are emotional arguments that almost never carry anything more than anecdotal evidence (and sometimes not even that).

Even a cursory look at the evidence shows that gun control *does* work and that the NRA's solutions (more guns and more laws allowing civilians to use guns as a first recourse) have done *nothing* to reduce the contagion's spread. When guns are easier to obtain, and when civilians are encouraged to use them for self-defense, the result is more deadly violence, not less. When legislation makes firearms more difficult to obtain, there is a palpable reduction in homicide rates.[24]

Though we have little to expect from the Trump administration in the way of gun-control legislation, the next liberal in the Oval Office may be able to hit the ground running. Action is piling up at the state level, and the calls for national legislation are growing louder by the day. According to Giffords Law Center, there were 1,638 firearm-related bills introduced in 2018, and a total of 67 gun-violence–reduction bills were signed into law in 2018. These included new gun-control laws in deep red states. Bump stocks were banned in Florida; background-check requirements were either added or beefed up in Florida, Louisiana, and Tennessee; laws designed to prevent domestic abusers from obtaining firearms were passed in Louisiana and Kansas; extreme-risk–protection orders (laws allowing either law enforcement, family members, or even members of the community to petition to have firearms confiscated from an at-risk individual) were introduced in Florida.[25] Not only are sensible gun controls moving through state legislatures, but measures designed to fight fire with fire are also being struck down: in Missouri, a strong common-sense campaign resulted in the defeat of a handful of bills designed to arm teachers and to allow guns in bars, childcare facilities, hospitals, and polling places.[26]

The public (or at least a sizable percentage of it) is at least starting to see the NRA's transparent jingoism for what it is. Collectively, we're starting to hear the false note struck when the NRA's representatives lean on their favorite adage: guns don't kill people, people kill people (the NRA has been trotting this one out each time somebody does something awful with a gun for at least six decades—perhaps longer). We know that this bad-faith argument neglects the ease with which a gun allows us to take a life. A knife can be an implement of death, as can a sturdy board or even a clenched fist, but none of these is remotely effective from across the street; none of these can snuff out a light in an instant with no more strength than it takes to strike a match.

We've started to hear the false note in their largely imaginary descriptions of good guys with guns who, apparently, are America's last and best line of defense against mass shooters. In only 3.1 per cent of the active-shooter incidents were the shooters stopped by a "good guy with a gun" (13.1 per cent of incidents were defused by unarmed civilians; more than half of the active shooters profiled ended the shootings themselves, either by fleeing the scene, surrendering, or committing suicide—this does not include those who committed *suicide by cop*).[27] The NRA would say that this shows we need *more* guns, but we're starting to see those arguments for what they are.

As those around us arm themselves to the teeth (with the average owner of an assault rifle owning at least three of them), the need for self-protection begins to feel more pressing, and, when those in our communities are armed with semi-automatic rifles (perhaps converted into all-but-fully-automatic machine guns), there is an understandable pull toward self-armament, especially among vulnerable communities that have been the target of escalating hate crimes. Thanks to the NRA's transparent alignment with the Republican Party and its willingness to demonize and scapegoat black communities (my hometown of Chicago being the most obvious example), black Americans justifiably feel themselves to be an uneasy fit with the NRA, but this doesn't mean that they are leaving the shooting or even the shooting clubs to white folks. The National African American Gun Association (NAAGA), with over 25,000 members at last count, has offered a place for black Americans to learn to shoot and to find solidarity with other black gun owners. Trump's America has seen emboldened white supremacists and, perhaps unsurprisingly, there has been a surge of interest in the organization since Trump's election, going from 14 chapters to 52 across America since his inauguration.

Black Americans have, of course, a complicated history with guns and, more particularly, with the Second Amendment and its defenders. There is a feeling in the black community—and a justified one—that the NRA is not interested in protecting black bodies or preserving black Second Amendment rights. They have held up Black Lives Matter as an example of the kind of dangerous organization that Americans need to arm themselves against. They traffic in racist dog whistles—we know what they mean when they talk about Chicago; we know what word they would rather use when they call us "thugs." They pay lip service to equal rights for all gun owners, but they have shown a moral duplicity by their silence in the wake of the case of Philando Castile, a licensed gun owner who was shot to death by a Minnesota police officer. NRA spokesperson Dana Loesch said that Castile was to blame for his own death because he had marijuana in the car. The group has, over and over again, made it crystal clear that blue lives matter more to them than black ones. Each time there is a controversial shooting, the NRA finds a way to blame the victim if they are black, either for carrying a gun or for not carrying a gun: "If innocent unarmed black men [...] are shot, it's because they lack firearms; if innocent black men who are armed [...] are shot, it's because they had a gun. Heads, you're dead; tails, you're also dead."[28] Over and over again, they stand up for those who take black lives in either an official or an unofficial capacity (they held up George Zimmerman, who shot Trayvon Martin, as a model gun owner, for example). They are, make no mistake about it, the militant wing not only of the Republican Party but also of white America and white supremacist America—and the line between these is growing fainter by the day.

Though we may (slowly—painfully slowly) be starting to see through the NRA's messaging, the American love of guns remains largely unchanged. Our love of the gun and all it stands for is, without doubt, a defining feature of America. We may never cast this off entirely. Our love of guns is here to stay, and this tells us more than we might wish known about our perpetual adolescence, about our fragile egos and particularly our fragile masculinity. The NRA and Fox pundits tell their viewers that manliness is under attack from every angle. Whiny libs, so they say, want men to be second-class citizens (they tip their hand frequently enough when they say the libs want men to be no different from women). Any challenge to male supremacy and to the ideas at the root of that supremacy must be resisted with hypermasculine displays of virility. Want to stick it to the liberals? Buy a gun. Want to show the leftists that your manhood is intact? Buy a big gun, a deadly gun. Even better, brandish this weapon in public. It's your right. Hold your weapon in your hand. Show the whole world what a big man you are (as long as you are not black or brown).

The comparison between male members and guns is not inapt. We want to believe that we hold power in our hands when we stand with our feet spread, our weapons extended. The gun is the great equalizer. It makes the small man feel as big as the large one, and it makes the large one feel like a king. No wonder so many of us bristle at the mere mention of gun restrictions. They are the tether that connects us to some shred of old-fashioned manhood; take them away, and we must deal with the world without something that guarantees our superiority. Take them away and we are naked and vulnerable, and the American male is never, and can never be, vulnerable.

The taking of a life remains, for some, the ultimate symbol of virility. The caged hunt, the dentist with the lion's head adorning the wall of his study, these things show man's attempt to grasp at the straw of his manhood, at older, more primitive notions of masculinity that demand a blood sacrifice. Ask the man who keeps a loaded pistol beneath his pillow or in his nightstand and he will, almost invariably, tell you it is for protection—to protect his property and his family, he will, he says, take a life without a second thought. Listen when he tells you how and why he will do this. It is not a horror barely to be imagined. It is engorged fantasy, the consummation of virile manhood, the king protecting his castle and chattel with fire and steel.

The voices of men like these are amplified in the gun debate. Instead of their voices, we need to start letting the dead enter the debate. The dead can't speak, but they can still have a politically charged voice. The Greeks called this *prosopopeia*—when the names of the dead are evoked as examples of sacrifice and suffering. We do this today with our hash tags, with *I am Eric Garner* printed on shirts, and with our use of the names of the dead to connect ourselves and our audience with our innocent dead. Obama: "If I had a son, he would have looked like Trayvon." This naming is a crucial part of our act of public mourning. Numbers have swelled beyond reckoning, and we need to descend to particulars in order to, as Simon Stow says in *American Mourning: Tragedy, Democracy, Resilience*, break these events down "into their constitutive parts"[29] to show not just the scope of these tragedies on the community but also their impact on families. When we feel each victim as a tearing asunder of a family, a removal of a father, a brother, a sister, a mother, a friend, our blood must seethe and roil beneath our skin. In the same way, we must (as some medical professionals have forced us to do) confront the visceral with our own eyes, must see without flinching what bullets do to bodies. We must do this to make transparent the stories we tell ourselves about gun violence—stories about heroism and sacrifice. These stories allow us to live in unreal worlds in which the gun is merely a tool—a tool of murder but, more important, a tool of protection. We are wrapped up in these worlds and these stories, wrapped in our fantasies.

For as long as we remain wrapped up in these fantasies, we will remain in the gun lobby's thrall. The contagion will continue to spread, and the problem will grow larger with each passing year. When we speak of the last mass shooting, we know that there will be another one and another one on the road ahead. Without something drastic, we will never be able to speak of the next last shooting as *the last mass shooting*.

Notes

1   Many of the details that follow are recorded in Harold Schecter, *The Serial Killer Files: The Who, What, Where, How, and Why of the World's Most Terrifying Murderers* (New York: Ballantine Books, 2003).

2   "Young Veteran Goes Berserk Killing 12 at Camden, N.J.," *Leominster Daily Enterprise*, 6 September 1949.

3   Almost half a century earlier, in 1903, 30-year-old Gilbert Twigg opened fire with a shotgun on a crowd that had gathered for a concert, killing eight people before turning the gun on himself. Twigg has been called the first modern mass shooter (and he does fit the profile), but Unruh was the first to generate significant national press coverage—a hallmark of modern mass shooters.

4   E.g., universal background checks, a new (and permanent) assault-weapons ban, stricter regulations governing who can own guns and how they should be stored, etc.

5   This is not to say that there was no regulation of any kind. Nearly every state, for instance, had bans on concealed weapons in the nineteenth century, but it was left to the states to decide what to do about guns within their borders.

6   Nearly a century later, the tax is *still* $200.

7   Miller, it is worth noting, was a known bank robber. He would be found shot to death before the Supreme Court would arrive at its decision. See *United States v. Miller*, 307 U.S. 174 (1939).

8   "The Gun under Fire," *Time*, 21 June 1968.

9   Thirty years later, *Time* would use the same cover for an updated story on gun control, adding only the year below the title.

10 "The Gun under Fire."

11 S. Rosenfeld, "The NRA Once Supported Gun Control," *Salon*, 14 January 2013.

12 M. Powell, "The NRA's Call to Arms," *Washington Post*, 6 August 2000.

13 F. Fessenden, "They Threaten, Seethe and Unhinge, Then Kill in Quantity," *New York Times*, 9 April 2000.

14 J. Pete Blair, "A Study of Active Shooter Incidents in the United States between 2000 and 2013" (Washington, DC: Federal Bureau of Investigation, 16 September 2013).

15 A.J. Willingham and Saeed Ahmed, "Mass Shootings in America Are a Serious Problem—and These 9 Charts Show Just Why," *CNN*, 6 November 2017.

16 T. Dickinson, "All-American Killer: How the AR-15 Became Mass Shooters' Weapon of Choice," *Rolling Stone*, 22 February 2018.

17 Ibid.

18 A. Neklason, "The Columbine Blueprint," *The Atlantic*, 19 April 2019.

19 Fessenden, "They Threaten."

20 Ibid.

21 J. Ax and G. Cherelus, "After Las Vegas Massacre, 'Bump Stock' Is Hot Item at U.S. Gun Shops," 4 October 2017, https://ca.news.yahoo.com/las-vegas-massacre-bump-stock-hot-item-u-001444967--finance.html.

22 J. Skebba, "Bump Stocks Illegal Now, but Few, if Any, Local Owners Have Turned Theirs In," *Blade*, 13 April 2019.

23 "Read Trump's Speech Addressing the Parkland School Shooting," *CNN*, 15 February 2018.

24 Julian Santaella Tenorio et al., "What Do We Know about the Association between Firearm Legislation and Firearm-Related Injuries?," *Epidemiologic Reviews* 38.1 (2016): 140–57.

25 A. Anderman, "Gun Law Trend Watch: 2018 Year-End Review," Giffords Law Center to Prevent Gun Violence, 14 December 2018.

26 Ibid.

27 Blair, "A Study of Active Shooter Incidents."

28 A. Serwer, "The NRA's Catch-22 for Black Men Shot by Police," *The Atlantic*, 13 September 2018.

29 Simon Stow, *American Mourning: Tragedy, Democracy, Resilience* (Cambridge: Cambridge University Press, 2017), 51.

Chapter Five

A WAR OF WORDS

The Politicization of Hate Speech

WORDS, TO ECHO THE COMMON PLATITUDE, HAVE POWER. Some words, spoken at the right place and time, carry power that is vastly disproportionate to their customary meaning and produce effects that are unforeseeable even to their speaker.

On Christmas Eve, 1913, hundreds of people gathered to celebrate at a venue called the Italian Hall, a two-story commercial and recreational building in the small mining town of Calumet, Michigan. Most of them were Finnish-American copper miners who had been on strike for five months, seeking union recognition. The festivities, sponsored by the Ladies' Auxiliary of the Western Federation of Miners labor union, took place in the large assembly room that comprised the second floor of the building, which could be accessed only by a single steep stairway. On this night, and under these circumstances, one particular word would carry more power than any other and would snuff out the lives of 73 people. That word was *fire*.

Recent scholarship has identified the man who shouted that word as a member of the local "Citizens' Alliance," an anti-labor vigilante group already responsible for several acts of violence against strikers.[1] Many of the miners brought their wives and children to the party, and it was this latter group—the children—upon whom the heaviest toll would be levied, with 59 of them being trampled to death during the panicked stampede. Since the attendees were primarily friends and co-workers, many of the children who were killed presumably met their deaths under the heels of people who were familiar to them and who wished them no harm.

There was no fire, of course. There was only its linguistic sign— the lethal word itself—and the terrifying visions it conjured in the frenzied minds of the people who heard it. That's what words do: they conjure images, articulate intent, and spark ideas. They give humans the ability to transmit these things to each other, but also to amplify them, along with attendant emotions like love and excitement, fear and hate. As Rabbi Yehuda Berg put it, "Words are singularly the most powerful force available to humanity. We can choose to use this force constructively with words of encouragement, or destructively using words of despair. Words have energy and power with the ability to help, to heal, to hinder, to hurt, to harm, to humiliate and to humble."[2]

It was perhaps with the relatively recent Italian Hall disaster in mind, along with a handful of similar events during his lifetime, that Supreme Court Justice Oliver Wendell Holmes Jr. gave birth to the metaphor that would come to define, in the minds of most Americans, one of the most commonsense limits to free speech. That metaphor— "falsely shouting fire in a theatre and causing a panic" and usually paraphrased as *shouting fire in a crowded theater*—was part of the Court's unanimous opinion in 1919's *Schenck v. United States*, which was penned by Justice Holmes, and has since passed the lips of nearly every American who has engaged in a discussion about free speech.[3]

In truth, there are very few limits on free speech in America. *Schenck*, in which the Court ruled that the right to free speech did not protect Schenck from being tried and convicted for passing out leaflets urging young men to resist the draft, was later narrowed to prohibit only speech that would cause "imminent lawless action." Thus Mr. Schenck's actions would have been protected as free speech under the later case. America's free speech is often held out as the envy of the world, and in a world where speech, even in Western countries, is increasingly restricted in attempts to avoid offending certain segments of the population, the right of Americans to say whatever they please is indeed special. But free speech is not without its burdens.

It means that we can speak our minds without fear of government censorship, but it means that others can do the same, even if their minds are twisted by vile ideologies. A manifest example of the elasticity of American liberality regarding offensive speech can be found in its grudging tolerance of the infamous Westboro Baptist Church (WBC), a very small Kansas church whose members seek to torment the families of recently deceased service members by picketing their funerals, and whose vulgar, anti-homosexual sign verbiage is all the more shocking because it is often displayed by the dewy-eyed children of Westboro members. While rank-and-file citizens often react with outrage and occasionally even resort to violence against these most extreme beneficiaries of free speech, the justice system protects even the vilest speech so long as it doesn't incite imminent lawless action. In 2011, the Supreme Court overturned a $10-million judgment against WBC for defamation, citing free-speech grounds.[4]

Hate speech is free speech, so it is protected.[5] The fact that hate speech falls under the aegis of free speech does not mean it is free of consequence, however. It carries a price tag, usually in the form of outrage and censure from the general public whenever a perceived line is crossed by the speaker. Since the rise and partial success of the civil rights movement, this censure has been an effective check on some of the more odious forms of hate speech, like overtly racist or misogynistic rhetoric—but the efficacy of this check has been increasingly diluted in recent years with the advent of the internet and the growing primacy of social media in public life.[6]

One of the problems is that the public doesn't have a single cohesive standard for what constitutes "hate speech." We live in a culture where the very idea of hate speech is often wielded as a bludgeon against people who are not exhibiting any actual "hate." Younger generations, in particular, have developed a tendency to conflate hate speech with speech that offends them and have sometimes even gone to the extreme of claiming that offensive speech is tantamount to violence. In this view, the *intent* of the speaker doesn't matter. All that matters is the impact of that speaker's words, which of course will vary depending on the listener. The hate need not actually exist in the speaker's heart if it can be gleaned from the effect of the speaker's words.

This approach is problematic in a number of ways, most critically because it encourages a disregard for objective truth, the esteem of which is critical to the functioning of healthy debate within a democracy. Knowing what is meant, or better yet, historically understood by the speaker's words, may be exhausting, but the lack of such rigor regulates all speech as both offensive and hateful. Reacting to all offensive speech as if it were hateful or violent creates rising levels of toxicity in our national discourse. Anger fuels further anger—and more angry speech—at the expense of productive conversation, all of which has a chilling effect on our willingness to interact with each other in good faith on a meaningful level.

If intent is irrelevant, and if hate speech can be defined as anything that hurts someone's feelings or in any way marginalizes them, nearly anything a person says can be construed by someone as "hate speech." Not only does this shut down potentially meaningful conversation before it can begin, but it gives people who actually do promote and defend hate-speech ammunition to bolster their own claims to "truth" and "marginalization." In other words, a hair-trigger sensitivity that imagines hate speech everywhere can provide camouflage to real hate, backed by real intent. Perhaps in evaluating whether a particular speech act is hate speech, we ought to bear in mind John Stuart Mill's harm principle: "The only purpose for which power can be rightfully exercised over any member of a civilized community, against his will, is to prevent harm to others."[7]

Taking the notion of intent one step further, there are instances where vestiges of racial stereotypes have worked their way into our language and culture, words and phrases that are patently offensive but that don't rise to the level of hate because of people's lack of awareness. In the neighborhood I grew up in, it was common for haggling over price to include the admonition "stop Jewing me!"[8] Even as children, we would say this.

It goes without saying that this was an insensitive term that is based on a deeply hurtful stereotype. It is reprehensible, but that's not the point. The point is that, for young children who had heard this term bandied about by adults for as long as we could remember, there was not an ounce of hatred in our hearts when we used it. This cringeworthy phrase was, during my own childhood, linguistically flaccid. The same could be said of our use of the term "gyp," as in "stop gypping me," which we had no idea was a reference to the gypsies or Roma people.

Does the ubiquity absolve the speaker from the charge of racial animus?

The fact that such language is regularly challenged, and has been pushed to the fringe of society, is a good thing. The assumption that a person using such language as "jewing" or "gypping" harbors hatred for Jewish or Roma people would have depended on a misconstruction of the speaker's true intent. Even the most reprehensible terminology might be bereft of malice, depending on who is using the term and in what context. Only if the intent is to harm, offend, denigrate, or defame a group of people does it rise to the level of hate speech.

In a social climate charged with political polarization, hate speech flows freely. Hate speech serves to alienate and disassociate different types of people. It becomes a means to stridently assert one's identity and allegiances and encourage a state of conflict with a perceived "other." The state that hate speech encourages—strident divisiveness—would seem to have no place in a society that values democratic inclusiveness. After all, hate speech seeks to intimidate and marginalize its targets, establish them as foreign or undesirable, and push them away. A visceral response to hate speech seems to only encourage this sense of divisiveness, of "us vs. them." Nonetheless, hate speech, and the inflammatory exchanges it tends to create, remains protected under the First Amendment.

Though difficult for some people to accept, this state of affairs exists as a consequence of the constitutional right of freedom of speech. The First Amendment robustly protects the ability to publicly share even the most noxious of views, and for good reason. Freedom of speech exists as the primary and essential avenue for political advocacy. Without it, those in power could censor the rhetoric that organizes and inspires people to take action and confront injustice. In this sense, freedom of speech protects us all and exists as a vital part of our democracy. Freedom of speech as guaranteed in the Constitution also presupposes the concept of personal accountability. This allows for the protection even of speech that tacitly endorses violent activity, as seen in the decision of *Brandenburg v. Ohio*.[9]

In this case, the court ruled that the First Amendment protected the right of a KKK speaker who publicly threatened revenge for the perceived suppression of whites. If this statement inspired an audience member to later assault a black man, the Klansman speaker would suffer no consequences. Though his words may have served to inspire the act, he has no personal accountability for the behavior of another person.

This fact changes, however, along the narrow lines delineated for the suppression of speech. Though its protections are inclusive and broad, freedom of speech does have its limits. In *Brandenburg*, the Supreme Court outlined a scenario in which the government could, in fact, intervene and punish someone for their use of words and symbols. In the event that a speaker intentionally and immediately provokes an audience to violence, he or she has crossed the line into unlawful territory. This is called the "incitement standard." Additionally, in *Chaplinsky v. New Hampshire*, the Supreme Court established the exception for so-called "fighting words," or language used in a one-on-one confrontation intended to provoke violence.[10] Freedom of speech also does not cover language or symbols used to directly threaten a specific individual. These restrictions create obvious grey areas. For example, when does hate speech devolve into harassment? When does the use of loaded symbolism constitute a hate crime?

A recent incident in Glenelg, Maryland, can serve to illustrate these distinctions. On the final day of the 2018 school year, the principal of Glenelg High School arrived in the morning to find the campus broadly vandalized with racist graffiti. The principal, David Burton, is black. His institution is the only predominantly white school in its county. Police identified the vandals as four white males in Glenelg's graduating class. Alongside obscenities and crude depictions of penises, the graffiti included explicitly racist and inflammatory symbols and language. Blacks, Jews, and homosexuals were all targeted, as was Principal Burton himself. Local prosecutors quickly labeled the incident a hate crime, and the court found all four teens guilty. Two of the teenagers' attorneys invoked the First Amendment in an attempt to have the hate-crime charges reduced to simple vandalism.

The judge would not accept this and sentenced all four teens to varying amounts of probation, community service, and jail time.[11]

Hate crimes occur when prejudice against a particular group of people identified by their religion, sexual orientation, race, or other characteristic motivates violence or harassment against them. Though often invoked in criminal charges, hate crimes rarely result in prosecution. The reason for this is simple: prosecutors must prove in court that prejudice motivated the crime, but this is actually quite difficult to do. For example, in 2017, also in Maryland, a man who belonged to a white-supremacist Facebook group fatally stabbed a black college student.[12] The two did not know each other, nor was there any apparent motive. Nevertheless, officials declined to classify the incident as a hate crime. In the absence of a lengthy record of racist inclinations, or the explicit utterance of slurs in the course of the attack, any link between prejudice and intent becomes speculative. When it comes to hate crimes—and hate speech—specific intent represents the gold standard. In order to hit a defendant with the stiffer penalties associated with hate crimes, or to delineate between protected free speech and targeted harassment, one must prove intent. In other words, it falls to the judge and jury to peer into the mind and heart of the accused. When it comes to non-violent acts of expression and the use of inflammatory symbols, this word "intent" defines the grey area beyond the limits of free speech.

In addition, disparate outcomes make it even harder to identify hate crimes and speech. Communication is a two-way street, and words and symbols in transit from a speaker's mind can translate differently to an audience's understanding. For example, a Confederate flag could represent to one person Southern pride, and to another, racism. These distinct outcomes of communication can thus obscure intent and place the burden of proof for hate speech on the offended. The same goes for hate crimes: it is easy to interpret the stabbing of a black college student as an act of hate, but does this mean we must interpret all interracial violence as motivated by hate? Does the white thief who robs a black man's convenience store have racist intentions? Probably not. Therefore, the identification of intent for a violent act can have very different outcomes.

The intent of the Glenelg teens, however, shone clearly in their vandalism of the school. The use of explicitly racist symbols and language, combined with targeted slurs such as "BURTON IS A NIGGER," more than satisfied the criteria for a hate crime. In order for speech, even hate speech, to remain protected, the speakers must violate neither private property nor an individual's right to personal security. Since the teenagers both desecrated their school and singled out their principal with racist language, the First Amendment provided no defense.

As mentioned above, two of the defense attorneys invoked the First Amendment. This attempt further illustrates the muddiness of free speech and reveals the difficulties inherent in establishing a clear standard. The public display of symbols like swastikas, or the burning of crosses or American flags, can prove viscerally offensive. However, the Supreme Court ruled in the 1989 case of *Texas v. Johnson* that the use of offensive symbols in a public space occurs within the protections of the First Amendment.[13] This particular case invalidated laws in 48 states that prohibited the desecration of American flags. As a result, the decision allows white supremacists to publicly hoist swastikas, Klan members to burn crosses, and anti-war protesters to burn American flags, while enjoying protection from legal retaliation. The Glenelg students displayed their "speech" across the property of a school campus; this identified the incident not as an act of free speech but as criminal trespass and vandalism. Furthermore, they did not display these symbols before a general audience but instead targeted their black principal. This distinction further distances their activity from the protections of free speech and glosses their "senior prank" with the ugly veneer of a hate crime.

At least one of the accused also put forth ignorance as a defense for his actions. Though he understood that the symbols and language he used were inflammatory, he claimed not to know the historical context that makes the swastika and KKK symbolism so viscerally hurtful. This ignorance defense represents a common strategy for those engaged in the use of offensive symbolism. Another is the appropriation of a symbol on limited grounds, as if one can pick and choose inherent meanings. For example, it's common to hear that the Confederate flag can simply illustrate "Southern pride," without any racist connotations. This strategy attempts to shift blame for offense away from the deployer of the loaded symbol and onto the shoulders of the offended.

The problem with the former defense, that of ignorance, is its inherent hollowness. In the case of the Glenelg teens, one must turn a blind eye to the fact that their teachers covered the Holocaust and KKK as part of normal coursework. Also, to pick and choose the connotations of a symbol is an act of bad faith against free speech. In this case, free speech becomes an act of subterfuge, in which symbols universally understood as offensive are utilized in a one-sided attack. In other words, an offender can communicate something intentionally hurtful, disavow responsibility for the offense, and place blame on the audience. Free speech thus becomes a way to dictate a dialogue or set the terms of understanding in a way that limits truly free speech. Speech is only free if universally so. If a person tries to control the terms of dialogue through the selective appropriation of loaded symbols, they disavow the notion of free speech. Regardless of the justification for use of an offensive symbol, it's impossible to control subsequent reactions. Symbols like the swastika or Confederate flag are thus beyond this selective appropriation. Regardless of the supposed reason for their use, they will always communicate hatred and racism.

When it comes to free speech, each of these strategies—ignorance and selective appropriation—represents an attempt to obscure intent. Since it is impossible to establish an objective standard for the use of racist language and symbols, it falls on the judicial system to define the limits of free speech on a case-by-case basis. In the case of the Glenelg teens, the judge saw through the defense arguments and handed out criminal penalties for a hate crime. It is important for everyone in our society to understand the reasons for this. A polarized political environment is defined through the everyday confrontation of violently opposing viewpoints. The difference between protected free speech and criminal hate speech not only frames these debates but also permits their existence in the public space as the only pathway toward mutual understanding.

This distinction is worth drawing because by characterizing every graceless idiom and every slip of the tongue as "hate speech," and by demanding that society react with the same groundswell of righteous indignation, we are increasing the signal-to-noise ratio and desensitizing ourselves to real hate speech when it occurs.

While the idioms from my childhood had their origins in an objectively awful stereotype, the propensity to assign malicious intent to offhand comments has become an all-too-common occurrence. In March 2019, Minnesota congresswoman Ilhan Omar fired off a tweet about Israeli influence on the Republican Party, saying "it's all about the Benjamins baby." The resulting backlash painted her as, among other things, anti-Semitic, thereby equating her words with the worst rant of the most dedicated neo-Nazi.

Minnesota Congresswoman Ilhan Omar.

It is not my intention to defend either Representative Omar or her choice of words but rather to point out how quickly and decisively the Twittersphere assigned malicious intent to both. It is impossible to know what was in her mind as she composed and posted her tweet, but its content was offhand and imprecise enough to serve as a cogent example of my point. The least charitable interpretation of her tweet is that she, a Muslim, considers Jews to be tight-fisted, or is at least willing to publicly traffic in that well-worn and hurtful trope. The most charitable interpretation, however, would be that she was casually using a line from an old Puff Daddy song as a device to bemoan the influence of money in America's foreign-policy decisions. This was, in fact, her subsequent defense, although of course that defense was offered after she had been accused of malicious intent. Weaponizing hate speech—or, in this case, weaponizing what appears to be the nebulous specter of hate speech—is nothing new. What *is* new is the situation we find ourselves in, and the contribution of this sort of bad-faith political wrangling to the rapid decline in the tone of our nation's political discourse.

If the GOP were really so offended by hate speech, and if intent is the key component of hate speech, then their actions would be markedly different. It is not only a fiery invective that reveals what is in the speaker's heart, after all. US Representative Steve King (R-Iowa), for instance, has long used chillingly allusive language such as "other people's babies" to signal his revulsion for people who don't look like him. This elected official's loathing of non-whites is overt and unmistakable and has been in evidence for many years.[14] Yet his fellow Republicans voted to censure him only recently, after nearly two decades in Congress, and then only as a concession to mounting public pressure. This contrasts with their swift and gleefully severe reaction to Omar's comparatively innocuous comment and is the very definition of bad faith in American politics, placing the value of temporary victory on social media over the value of truth itself.

They're not the only ones, however. On the other side of the aisle, many reactions to Omar's tweet seemed conspicuously reactionary as well, even if the motivations were less overtly political. Democrats rushed to express anger over the tweet and to support the Congressional resolution that indirectly condemned her words.[15] While their umbrage was perhaps genuine, in the absence of any real intent behind Omar's words, that umbrage was misplaced. This brand of reflexive outrage is potentially harmful to the cause of conquering real anti-Semitism. Worse, it cheapens our discussion of hate speech in general, diluting the very meaning of the term.

Supporting a toothless resolution in order to state the obvious might score temporary political points, but given the long-term adulteration of such empty and disingenuous gestures with regard to the fight against real hate speech, it also rises to the level of bad-faith politics. What if there were more to this conversation? More important, what if everyone had first assumed that Omar's statement was innocent, instead of immediately suspecting otherwise? What if, instead of a nation of mind-readers, we were a nation of people who operated under the default assumption that others—even those with opposing political or ideological viewpoints—were acting in good faith and were in fact motivated not by hatred and malice but by their own conception of morality, at least until proven otherwise? In this age of instantaneous communication and widespread dissemination of information, what kind of elevated discussion might ensue?

In other words—as preposterous as this might sound in the current climate—what if America could adopt a norm in which our first inclination was to give each other the benefit of the doubt?

How different might our national discourse sound, and our political landscape look? Consider a white college student who feels alienated from the "browning" of America. Is there any rational way to conceive of that alienation without rooting it in deep-seated, or even shallow-seated, racism? Xenophobic fear of the other is an older and deeper psychological condition than racism, so we know that the two are related but not identical. After 400 years of intertwining in American culture, however, is it possible to distinguish and separate them from one another in a way that does not do violence to history, especially the lived historical truths of African Americans and other subalterns? What if that student focused instead on her own whiteness and how it was socially and historically constructed?

There are a few things preventing this, of course.

Identity politics, increasingly embraced by people on both sides of the ideological spectrum, is part of the problem. The dangers are fairly clear, for any willing to look: a rise in identity politics on one side, which then fuels a surge in identity politics on the other side, inevitably leads to a Balkanization of society. Also clear is that the increasing polarization in our society and the global rise in populism over the last decade coincides with an increasing emphasis on identity politics.[16]

What is less clear is what can be done about it. While identity politics is inherently divisive in that it carves out groups of people based on shared differences, it is also a vital tool for marginalized and underrepresented groups. Any critique of identity politics must recognize and grapple with the historical fact that white people invented "race" and racial identity politics during the colonization of the New World as a weapon to hold down recently enslaved black people.[17] Thus, as historian David Roediger has argued, because white people have invested so much value into "whiteness," many of them consider it to be the most valuable property they own.[18] When black people eventually fashioned politics out of their racial identity, they were turning around the weapon of race upon its creators. In this light, would it make sense for black people to abandon racial identity politics before whites have at least begun to do so first?

On the national stage, groups band together in this way on all sorts of levels, from race to religion to sexual orientation, and various identity groups can form alliances with each other, increasing their influence still further. It is difficult to imagine that the monumental social progress over recent decades could have occurred in the absence of this approach. If, for example, a corporation that employs mostly males tends to discriminate to the detriment of its female employees, those female employees can increase their influence and precipitate change more rapidly only by banding together and addressing the problem with one voice.

There is strength in numbers, and this has been a recognizable reality throughout human history. A solitary pastor marching in Montgomery, Alabama, in 1956, for instance, would have gone unnoticed, but a motivated, like-minded multitude was impossible to ignore. This led to change that could never have been achieved without a narrow recognition of shared identity. However, that change also relied upon an appeal to common humanity. The street politics of narrow identity were essential to organizing Montgomery's black populace so that it could find the courage to act collectively, but success ultimately rested as well on an aspirational politics of broad "human" identity that promised to embrace everyone in Montgomery regardless of race.

Deindividuation, "the situation in which individuals act in groups and do not see themselves as individuals [which] facilitates the elicitation of suppressed behaviors, which may transgress social norms,"[19] can be a valuable tool, giving marginalized groups a voice and a way to assert their own interests. Collective action is unimaginable without some degree of deindividuation, but that does not mean that collective action is irrational.[20] Like any powerful tool—fire, for instance— deindividuation can be dangerous as well.

Human history is replete with examples of how deindividuation can lead to dehumanization. Some such examples are deeply painful to contemplate, from centuries-spanning horrors like colonialism and slavery to specific atrocities like the Holocaust or the Reign of Terror, each of which required that the perpetrator view his victims as a group instead of as thinking, feeling individuals worthy of kindness and empathy.

Deindividuation has another catch as well. It can be applied to others, to dehumanize them, but we can also apply it to ourselves to absolve us of responsibility for our own actions. Military training relies heavily on both of these aspects of deindividuation, systematically stripping recruits of their sense of self and replacing it with a sense of unity and camaraderie, while also stripping adversaries of their humanity and replacing that humanity—to some extent, at least—with something that deserves to be killed when the order is given.

Identity politics does not deindividuate people to this degree, but the lesson still applies. At some level, in order for our nation to function in a way that is productive and beneficial to all, these divisions must melt away and all identity-centered groups must allow themselves to coalesce with society at large. By society at large, I do not mean society as it exists now, in its basically white-supremacist form. The idea is not that black people must conform themselves to a white-defined concept of society, nor the opposite; it is that *both* black and white people would allow those race-based identities to recede in importance as compared to a newly created, overarching, non-racialized national identity. Their individual members must also re-individuate, for reasons discussed below.

This is something that should happen naturally, since individuals have a wide range of interests and concerns, many of which are common to a broader range of people than those in their primary identity group. Historically, the necessity of coexisting in the real world has provided impetus to seek out commonality and maintain some level of social integration with broader society. With the advent of the internet, however, that requirement has been diminished considerably. It is easier than ever to find large groups of people with whom we agree, and even easier to isolate ourselves from viewpoints that conflict with our own.

Facebook's early aspiration to "connect the world" might have sounded like a splendid idea when Mark Zuckerberg first gave voice to it, but now that billions of us actually *are* connected on his platform, Zuckerberg's notion of a shiny online Shangri-la has lost much of its luster. Connecting everyone online, it turns out, can have dire consequences in the real world. One of those consequences is the amplification of hate speech.

Facebook's role in the 2016 presidential election is well known. It served as a willing platform for political bile and targeted misinformation on a level that has never been seen before, providing foreign enemies with a toxic IV drip connected directly to mainstream America. Race also served to inspire the intent of misinformation campaigns. During the presidential campaign, Trump polled poorly among black voters. A voter's race subsequently served to make them a recipient of misinformation, as Russia directly targeted blacks in its Facebook campaigns. Under the influence of this false information, a black could then place a vote under false pretenses and help elect someone antagonistic to their interests. Targeted misinformation campaigns can therefore serve as components of institutionalized racism.

What is less widely discussed, however, is that Facebook's business model itself is predicated upon favoring divisive political content above the high-minded dialogue some may have envisioned when Zuckerberg promised to connect everyone to each other. It's a simple model, in the end: Facebook's revenue comes from targeted advertising, where engagement is the primary selling point to advertisers. In days of yore, engagement meant addictive online games like Farmville and Mafia Wars. Today, however, the most powerful emotional driver of engagement is good old-fashioned outrage. While the company must at least appear to care about the problem, therefore—offering various fixes and instituting new policies and vetting procedures—actually fixing the problem happens to run afoul of its core incentive, which is to generate advertising revenue.[21] That revenue is staggering, providing powerful incentive to ignore or justify the toxic effect that Facebook has on our national discourse, in much the same way as many in Congress ignore or justify the toxic effect of their "anti-Semitism" rhetoric.

Although it is almost impossible to measure the volume of online hate speech with any precision, Facebook, Twitter, and YouTube are by far the largest online purveyors of hate speech—wittingly or otherwise—simply by virtue of their massive user bases.[22] Twitter—which, unlike Facebook, allows user anonymity that seems to embolden some of our worst instincts—is notorious for its outrage-mongering trolls. Google, through its property YouTube, offers a smorgasbord of videos containing all manner of hate and rancor. Reddit, whose upvote system tends to bury unpopular speech on its more highly frequented subreddits, nonetheless contains its fair share of user-generated bile.

In other words, hate speech is everywhere, converging upon us from all sides. To retain our sanity without going offline completely, many understandably feel that they *must* limit their interaction to like-minded people, and that they *must* exclude those who disagree with them. The alternative, due to the sheer volume of information involved, is utter exhaustion.

* * *

With only a 12-month exception in 2007 and a three-year stint at an Historically Black College or University in Ohio, I have taught at colleges that are small, private, and white-church–affiliated. Being the only African American (in one situation) and one of only three in two others, I have found myself in the middle of campus controversies concerning allegations of hate speech and hate acts and the ensuing debates about free speech, free assembly, and the difference between intent and impact. For example, when an organization practices certain slave rituals as a way to teach the horrors of slavery and promote understanding, some may claim that to be re-traumatizing, insensitive, and terrorizing both to participants and to those in whom they confide. If a middle-class, white, heterosexual man gets frustrated and creates a straight-white-male club, he may be told it is fueled by hate even though the student, who feels marginalized himself, wants to align with similar students.

Likewise, members of that group, along with some in the class of females and maybe non-heterosexuals and even some blacks, might say, "why do we still have black history month?" It is clear that students of color and most liberals will clamor and rally around such a question as hate-full and causing black students to be unappreciated, while it might in fact be a feeling of white isolation or lack of particular attention within this identity game of politics. Campuses are forced to wrestle with these questions and attempt to create state-ments of conduct to protect marginalized groups while, contempora-neously, wielding a free-speech arsenal for the "majority population."

And so the fractures remain, and our divisions deepen, and our affinity for identity politics becomes ever more entrenched. That aforementioned necessity—to melt into society, and to find a measure of commonality with those with whom we disagree—has faded into the background. We are free to confine our interactions to people of our choosing, never having to grapple with the notion that Americans who see things differently from us might not be our enemies and might not be acting from malice or stupidity but might simply be consulting a different moral matrix.[23]

In this climate, we are also free to reconstruct any of our fellow Americans into a form that best fits our preferred narrative and to scrutinize their every utterance in the hopes of finding something that will authenticate the effigy we have built. When we do find such confirmation, we can vent our spleen immediately, and even anony-mously if we wish. But this is not how a healthy democracy oper-ates. Moreover, it does not seem to be an environment in which any democracy, healthy or otherwise, can long sustain itself.

Whichever side of the political divide we happen to be on, it is easiest to blame the other for this state of affairs. Each side, left and right, has its authoritarian elements, more concerned with conformity than with free speech, and each of these extremes presents ready fod-der for the other side to use in an attempt to broad-brush the opposi-tion. The political center, once an oasis of sanity in America's two-party system, is rapidly becoming a desert, an uninhabitable no-man's land where reasoned non-extremists go to die in obscurity.

But what if it were different? What if there were a way to bridge the chasm? Again—though preposterous—what if America could adopt a norm where, instead of assuming the most damaging inter-pretation of a statement or position to be true, our inclination was to give each other the benefit of the doubt? What if we fought the erroneous assertion that life is a battle between good people and evil people, and assumed instead that those who oppose us do so in good faith? At least, again, until they provide evidence to the contrary.

This might sound implausible, but drastic adaptation is necessary. We are in uncharted territory, and the situation is increasingly
desperate.

On the right, well-sourced facts are derided as fake news, science
is regarded with suspicion, and humankind's most primitive fears are
exploited, magnified, and weaponized by the political elite. Driven
by fear of obsolescence and a yearning for a bygone America that
never really existed—at least not for all Americans—the right has
shed its pretentions to conservatism and has embraced the only people left who will pretend to listen to their concerns: the power-hungry
populists. There is a new freedom on the right, and it is the freedom
to hate openly. While, to be fair, the majority on the right do not
exercise this freedom, they too often seem content to bask in its glow.

One way in which we deindividuate others is by imprinting them
with the label "stupid," and it is often easy to do this with right-leaning
people, especially in the era of Facebook, where obviously false claims
and stories so easily gain traction. But it's not necessarily stupidity
at play here. One feature of basic tribalism is that people willingly
embrace obvious empirical untruths in order to signal their loyalty
and demonstrate their commitment to their group—and to the larger,
metaphorical Truth that the group or movement represents.

There's also a level of visceral glee involved, which transcends
empirical truth in the same way that pro wrestling does, providing
spectacle instead of substance. Truth doesn't really matter: only the
spectacle does, along with the reaction of the opposition. Donald
Trump understands this fact and exploits it regularly, which is why
American public life often feels like an episode of a particularly toxic
reality-television show. But Trump isn't the cause here—he is a symp-
tom, someone who figured out how to exploit our new reality for
his own benefit. If he were gone tomorrow, the societal terrain upon
which his methods found purchase would still remain, and others on
the right would find a way to fill the vacuum.

On the left, the problem is less about overt hate than it is about
the aforementioned conflation of hate speech with anything that is
deemed offensive or hurtful, and the resulting lack of tolerance for
dissenting viewpoints. The overtly authoritarian inclination of far-
right ideology is, when mirrored on the far left, more subtle, but still
clearly present. Authoritarianism is a human impulse, after all.

On the internet in particular, and especially in the left-leaning parts of the Twittersphere, the aforementioned disregard for intent when it comes to defining hate speech seems to have ingrained itself particularly deeply, resulting in the inclination to seize upon the most damning interpretation of someone's words and to amplify that interpretation with little regard for the true intent of the speaker, all too often creating a viral backlash that does immense harm not only to the reputation of the speaker but also to the well-being of political dialogue in general.

Perilous times indeed.

But again, what if things were different? What if we decided to ascribe moral motivations to everyone as a matter of course? What if we were to make offensive speakers prove that they actually *are* racists, or misogynists, or hate-mongers, rather than assuming they are by default and then demanding that they prove otherwise?

The overwhelming majority of the actors described above, whether on the right or left of the ideological spectrum, want the same things, like security, peace, and prosperity for their children. Understanding this core reality, and forcing ourselves to extend empathy to the people with whom we most fervently disagree, is one of the obligatory requirements for regaining our self-image as a single people, and as a single, uniquely visionary nation, united and strong in spite of our deep and innumerable differences. We must somehow regain the ability to value truth above all else and to elevate that truth above our reflexive embrace of moral pageantry.

We now live, it sometimes seems, in the midst of a perpetual stampede not unlike that frenzied exodus in 1913 from the Italian Hall in Calumet, Michigan. The word *fire* has been shouted, and we are all intent on repeating it, and reacting to it, often without regard for whether or where the fire actually exists, or for its real causes, or for the potentially catastrophic consequences of our mad dash toward an exit that doesn't exist. While the outlook often seems bleak, there is hope.

As a species, we have transcended our primitive origin like no other species we know of. Through scientific progress, we have transcended our biological limitations, rendering insignificant many physical limitations, like poor eyesight or missing limbs, which would have been fatal in a purely Darwinian context. We have also been successful, at times, in muting certain traits, innate impulses such as tribalism and fear of change—instinctual ramparts that served us well during the infancy of human civilization but that now obstruct our vision and our forward progress—and might ultimately threaten our long-term survival.

Much attention has been paid to the selfish nature of the human species, and such self-interest certainly does exist and can often be sated only at the expense of others. Slavery, which has existed since the dawn of history, is this propensity for self-interest writ large. But we must also recognize that humans are inherently social creatures, and from a biological standpoint we have evolved to work well with each other and to expand our groups into larger and larger networks. We have also evolved all the traits necessary to build functional societies, to love each other, to care about our fellow man, and to have meaningful friendships.

Humanity currently finds itself in a new and dramatically expanded social context, where connectivity is suddenly absolute and information—accurate or not, relevant or not—is more freely disseminated than ever before. We have not evolved to handle this, which is presumably part of the cause of the tumultuous times that have been thrust upon us, but we have shown, time and again, that we are an adaptive species. We have also shown that we have the ability to extend our social group indefinitely, from a tribe to a village to a city to a nation, so there is no reason to believe we cannot acclimatize ourselves to these new circumstances too, if we understand the need for it. We can enlarge the tent, but to do so we must be willing to empathize and forgive.

For instance, we can retain the positive attributes of identity politics, such as the increased allotment of power to the marginalized, while working to minimize its negative effects, such as division and isolation. All that is required is a shift from an emphasis on a common enemy to an emphasis on our common humanity. We need to do something that Americans have shown themselves uniquely capable of doing, which is embracing both our shared identity and our own individuality. Instead of viewing ourselves as social groups, we should view ourselves as individuals on the small scale and Americans—human beings, even—on the larger scale, subordinating but not erasing the distinctions in between.

The danger to minority groups and nonconformists generally is that the process of subsuming themselves to a "shared identity" could become a process of assimilation into a set of white-defined cultural norms. One way of preventing this is to adopt David Hollinger's "post-ethnic" perspective, where ethnic stands for social particularities of varying kinds: "a post-ethnic perspective ... recognize[s] that most individuals are involved in many ... communities simultaneously and that the carrying out of any person's own life-project entails a shifting division of labor between the several 'we's' of which the individual is a part. How much weight is assigned to the fact that one is Pennsylvania Dutch or Navaho, relative to the weight assigned to the fact that one is also an American, a molecular biologist, a woman, and a Baptist?"[24]

How those "weights" are assigned depends on how important to one's life a given identity seems to be, which in turn depends in large part on how persons identifying differently treat one. This means that as long as white people mistreat black people on the basis of skin-color prejudice, racial identity will remain very important to both groups, whether they like it or not.

If this sounds unwieldy or dichotomous, regard what is surely among the most famous lines uttered in the last century, where Dr. Martin Luther King Jr. articulated his vision of a nation where a person would be judged not by the color of his skin but by the content of his character. King surely knew that the utopia he was invoking—a nation where *everyone* viewed *everyone else* in terms of their individual merit—was a stark impossibility, given human nature. Equally obvious, then, is that his exhortation—like that of many great speakers and sermonizers—was aimed not at society as a whole but at the individual hearer, whose power to affect change was limited primarily to his own actions.

The "nation" King referred to, in the most practical sense, was not some far-off neverland but a state of being that was immediately attainable on the individual level. While he presumably did hope that such a literal nation would eventually come to be, surely his immediate concern was with the people to whom he was speaking at that moment. In this context, his message was clear: each person listening to his words could create a tiny version of his nation simply by putting the stated principle into action. Combined, these individual changes could create societal change, but it had to start with the individual.

King was a master practitioner of identity politics, but he also seemed to sense that there was a point where identity politics must reach the limit of its usefulness. Identity politics may serve as a foundation, giving voice to marginalized *groups*, but in doing so identity politics would necessarily subsume King's *individual* whose worth is to be judged.

To put it in simpler terms, King clearly eschewed, in word and deed, the focus on a common enemy and appealed instead to a focus on our common humanity. This is what we must do today. And in order to be both meaningful and truly uniting, this conception of our common humanity must be based on the views and values of all Americans, not just white ones. In other words, we need a project of redefining our common humanity in a way that transcends racial division and creates a powerful new sense of national or human identity capable of transcending and overcoming the old, race-based identities. One encouraging aspect of this apparent dichotomy is that America itself has always placed value on both the individual and the collective populace. Other democratic nations tend to base their national ethos on equality and fraternity—as does America—but stop short of placing importance on the individual.

Somewhere, buried amid all our internecine strife, and amid all the disparate groups that comprise America, there is a uniquely American understanding that the individual matters. There are extremes—on one side that the individual should be subsumed by the greater national identity, and on the other side that consideration of the individual deserves primacy over all else—but neither of these extremes is workable in any practical sense. To survive, we must find a way to embrace both simultaneously, and to do that we must transcend our propensity for tribalism.

We prefer to believe that we have relegated such impulses to the periphery, but they still exist and have grown stronger since 2016. As we have seen in recent years, they still smolder beneath the surface, and they still flare within us when we feel threatened, and they still have the power to consume us if we allow them to burn unchecked. These impulses make us susceptible to those who would use bad-faith political tactics to exploit us. The unfortunate part is that, as with the disaster in Calumet, no actual fire need exist for these impulses to do damage. The threat alone—conveyed through words born of fear and impelled by an intent to inflame—is enough to do us harm by compelling us to harm one another, even in contravention to our own best interests, and of our own future.

Our challenge as a democratic citizenry—as urgent a biological imperative to modern humanity as warmth and shelter once were to our forebears—is to lay bare the folly of those among us who, in their own capitulation to these impulses, would start a stampede that would crush the better angels of our nature beneath the panicked heels of the antediluvian demons we pretend to have banished.

We already know one way to oppose this deluge of hatred and fear, and how to prevail against it. The wisest and bravest among us, from Mohandas K. Gandhi to Martin Luther King Jr., have provided us with real-life demonstrations by lying down in front of that deluge and letting it wash over them, often at steep personal cost. In doing so, they have shown us the only practical way to deal with hate, and with the people who invoke it through anger and fiery invective.

Though it is difficult, particularly in this chaotic new social landscape we inhabit, we must deal with the fire of hatred not by further stoking its flames but by quenching them with a commitment to empathy and brotherhood, to fidelity and reason, and to calm, peaceful discussion, even when those around us seem compelled to feed themselves to its fury.

Notes

1   Steve Lehto, *Death's Door: The Truth Behind the Italian Hall Disaster and the Strike of 1913*, 2nd ed. (New York: Momentum, 2013).

2   See https://www.facebook.com/yehuda.berg/posts/160262703989960.

3   *Schenck v. United States*, 249 U.S. 47 (1919).

4   *Snyder v. Phelps*, 562 U.S. 443 (2011).

5   *Matal v. Tam*, 582 U.S. 137 S. Ct. 1744, 198 L.Ed.2d 366 (2017). See https://www.supremecourt.gov/opinions/16pdf/15-1293_1o13.pdf.

6   See *Contreras v. Crown Zellerbach*, 88 Wn.2d 735 (1977), 565 P.2d 1173 (Wash. S. Ct.): "As we as a nation of immigrants become more aware of the need for pride in our diverse backgrounds, racial epithets which were once part of common usage may not now be looked upon as 'mere insulting language.'"

7   John Stuart Mill, *On Liberty* (London, 1879), 23.

8   In the city of Chicago, the area that is home to the University of Illinois at

Chicago was, for decades, called Jew Town. Most of us from the South Side in the 1980s and 1990s assumed that it was just an innocuous term coined due to cheap prices/deals on clothes and other items.

9   J.L. Walker, "Brandenburg v. Ohio," *The First Amendment Encyclopedia*, https://www.mtsu.edu/first-amendment/encyclopedia. See also Mark E. Walker, "Order on Cross-Motions."

10 J.M. Bitzer, "Chaplinsky v. New Hampshire," *The First Amendment Encyclopedia*.

11 J. Contrera, "They Covered Their School in Racist Graffiti. They Apologized. But Will They Change?" *Washington Post*, 9 July 2019.

12 L. Bui, "Man Arrested in Fatal Stabbing at University of Maryland Will Not Face Federal Hate-Crime Charges," *Baltimore Sun*, 30 June 2019.

13 J.M. Bitzer, "Texas v. Johnson," *The First Amendment Encyclopedia*. This was also the stated basis for dismissing the defamation case against Westboro Baptist Church in 2011. See above, p. 000, note 0.

14 G. Trip, "A Timeline of Steve King's Racist Remarks and Divisive Actions," *New York Times*, 15 January 2019.

15 H. Res. 183, 116th Congress, 7 March 2019, states in pertinent part as follows: Resolved, That the House of Representatives—

   (1) rejects the perpetuation of anti-Semitic stereotypes in the United States and around the world, including the pernicious myth of dual loyalty and foreign allegiance, especially in the context of support for the United States-Israel alliance;

   (2) condemns anti-Semitic acts and statements as hateful expressions of intolerance that are contradictory to the values that define the people of the United States; ...

   (5) acknowledges the harm suffered by Muslims and others from the harassment, discrimination, and violence that result from anti-Muslim bigotry;

   (6) condemns anti-Muslim discrimination and bigotry against all minorities as contrary to the values of the United States; ....

16 Ian Bremmer, *Us vs. Them: The Failure of Globalism* (New York: Portfolio/Penguin, 2018).

17 Edmund S. Morgan, *American Slavery, American Freedom: The Ordeal of Colonial Virginia* (New York: W.W. Norton, 1975); Theodore W. Allen, *The Invention of the White Race*, 2 vols. (New York: Verso, 1997).

18 David R. Roediger, *The Wages of Whiteness*, rev. ed. (New York: Verso, 2007).

19 F. Vilanova et al., "Deindividuation: From Le Bon to the Social Identity Model of Deindividuation Effects," *Cogent Psychology* 4.1 (2017).

20 Caroline Kelly and Sara Breinlinger, *The Social Psychology of Collective Action: Identity, Injustice and Gender* (Abingdon, UK: Taylor and Francis, 1996); George Rudé, *The Crowd in History 1730–1848: A Study of Popular Disturbances in France and England* (London: J.J. Wiley & Sons, 1981).

21 Roger McNamee, *Zucked: Waking Up to the Facebook Catastrophe* (New York: Penguin 2019). The business model of Fox News likewise depends heavily on manufacturing selective outrage among its viewers. J. Allsop, "Fox News Draws Renewed Scrutiny—and Outrage," *Columbia Journalism Review*, 11 March 2019.

22 M. Mainack, L.A. Silva, & F. Benevenuto, "A Measurement Study of Hate Speech in Social Media," *Proceedings of the 28th ACM Conference on Hypertext and Social Media*, Prague, Czech Republic, 2017.

23 Jonathan Haidt, *The Righteous Mind: Why Good People Are Divided by Politics and Religion* (New York: Pantheon, 2012).

24 D. Hollinger, "How Wide the Circle of the 'We'? American Intellectuals and the Problem of the Ethnos since World War II," *American Historical Review* 98.2 (1993): 317–37.

Chapter Six

ORIGINS, INTENTIONS, AND MEANINGS

The Rebel Battle Flag and Its Role in Creating a Bad-Faith White Identity

TECHNICAL NOTE: THE CONFEDERATE FLAG THAT HAS become such a controversial symbol today was not the official flag of the Confederate government. The Confederacy's original "Stars and Bars" flag looked so similar to the "Stars and Stripes" that rebel soldiers were confused and sometimes fired on their own. To avoid confusion, Robert E. Lee's Army of Northern Virginia (ANV) created a square, red flag with a blue, spangled diagonal cross or saltire, similar to the Cross of St. Andrew that was familiar to soldiers of Scottish descent.[1] Eight decades later, in 1948, a rectangular version of the battle flag regained prominence as a symbol of protest against federal civil rights legislation.

Origins: Racism, Art, and Good Faith—
The Arnautoff and Crumpler Murals

Explaining the meaning of a symbol in verbal form necessarily does violence to it, since the broad range of cognitive and emotional responses evoked by an especially potent symbol like the rebel battle flag defy the often clumsy precision of language. Although the proposition that such meanings are socially constructed—and revised—over time is no longer controversial, specifically how this happens is a very complex matter. A recent and ongoing controversy over public art in San Francisco that some call racist can serve as a piquant entrée.

For the subaltern,[2] one generation's blow for freedom may seem timid or even retrograde to the next generation's cutting edge, who naturally chafe at the limits of past progress. Consider the case of Victor Arnautoff's 13-panel mural "The Life of George Washington," which was painted as a protest against racism yet now faces imminent destruction for allegedly being racially offensive itself.

Victor Arnautoff was a left-wing Russian émigré painter who took up mural painting as a way to speak truth to power, specifically on behalf of working people and people of color. From 1929 to 1931, he studied mural painting with the world's greatest muralist, Mexico's Diego Rivera, also a man of the Left. In 1936 Arnautoff was hired, via the Works Progress Administration (WPA), to paint a mural about George Washington at a new high school named after Washington in San Francisco.

At that time, history curricula provided a sanitized, whites-only version of US history. They heroized George Washington and other "founding fathers" while hiding these figures' roles as slave-owners and Indian killers. Working in the vein of social realism, Arnautoff visually subverted the whitewashed Washington by depicting the "Father of His Country" victimizing black slaves and Indians. According to historian and Arnautoff biographer Robert Cherny, the artist included images and scenes that spoke the truth while evading censorship:[3]

> In the murals, Arnautoff implicitly challenged the version of U.S. history then typical in American high schools. In depicting Mount Vernon, Arnautoff literally marginalized Washington and put enslaved African Americans in the center of one of the scenes. The mural presented a

counter-narrative to most high school histories of the time, which tended to ignore the existence of slaves at Mount Vernon, as well as the paradox of slaveholders fighting for the principle that all men are created equal. Another large mural presents Washington pointing the nation to the West. Again, however, Arnautoff's counter-narrative makes it dramatically clear that the way west was over the body of a dead Indian.[4]

As Cherny has pointed out elsewhere, Arnautoff deliberately placed subaltern Americans—blacks, Indians, workers—at the center of several scenes: "The center of the four largest murals are held by Native Americans, working-class revolutionaries, and enslaved African Americans." Arnautoff's mural makes clear that slave labor provided the plantation's economic basis and "the procession of spectral future pioneers move west over the body of a dead Indian, challenging the prevailing narrative that westward expansion had been into largely vacant territory."[5] At a time when even the existence of past racial oppression was hidden by the history books, Arnautoff's mural spoke truth to power about white supremacy.

By the 1960s, this sort of truth-telling had really gained steam, as black activists began to succeed in forcing recognition of the role played by racism in US history, but back at George Washington High School, black students wanted more. They wanted recognition, not only of their ancestors' victimization but also of their struggles to not be victimized. Viewing Arnautoff's depictions of oppression as celebrations thereof, in 1966 they organized a movement demanding the destruction of the mural. Eventually, however, they agreed to its preservation on the condition that a counterbalancing mural be added nearby.

The activists already had an artist in mind: Dewey Crumpler, a black 1967 graduate of San Francisco's Balboa High School. First shocked by the images of slaves and the dead Indian, Crumpler soon changed his mind and wished to supplement the Arnautoff mural. Initially denied the commission because of his youth and inexperience, Crumpler traveled to Chicago, New York, and Detroit to study mural painting, and he completed murals commissioned in Detroit and San Francisco. In 1970, he studied mural painting in Mexico City under its two greatest practitioners, Pablo O'Higgins and David Siqueiros, who had worked closely with Rivera and were familiar with Arnautoff. Finally, in 1971, the powers that be relented and commissioned

Crumpler to paint a three-panel mural at the high school, depicting the lives and struggles of black, brown, and red Americans, which remains in place today.

Now, 48 years later, the Arnautoff mural faces destruction, again because of its alleged racism. Ironically, Dewey Crumpler opposes the destruction of the Arnautoff mural, arguing not only that it is not racist but also that "my mural is part of the Arnautoff mural, part of its meaning, and its meaning is part of mine. If you destroy his work of art, you are destroying mine as well."[6] The two works of art, in other words, relate to one another intertextually as part of a single whole. In this light, the Crumpler mural seems less like a corrective to Arnautoff's and more like its obverse, a reminder that white supremacy created not only oppression but also the conditions for liberation movements among the oppressed.

Generally conceding that Arnautoff did not have racist intent, today's mural critics nonetheless argue that the negative impact of the mural on young people, namely that it creates a hostile environment for learning, outweighs the artist's intent. Indeed, the fact that the mural is located in a space designed for children—albeit ones on the cusp of adulthood—has allowed its critics to shelter their arguments under the rubric of child protection. Contrariwise, however, mural defenders argue that the mural presents an educational opportunity to help students learn how to understand a work of art beyond its initial emotional impact, how to read a work of art to see its deeper and more nuanced meanings.

Regardless of what one thinks about this issue, a reasonable observer reviewing the controversy is struck by the fact that both sides have advanced well-reasoned, evidence-based arguments, apparently made in a good faith effort to seek the public good. This is the kind of public-forum debate we need in a modern democracy. In this sense, the mural issue can serve as a useful contrast to our discussion of the rebel battle flag, where good faith is sometimes in short supply.

The Civil War and Its Causes

The question of the meaning of the Confederate flag necessarily refers back to the controversy over the meaning of the Confederacy itself. Why did the Southern states secede?

The Sons of Confederate Veterans website assures visitors today that "the citizen-soldiers who fought for the Confederacy personified the best qualities of America. The preservation of liberty and freedom was the motivating factor in the South's decision to fight the Second American Revolution. The tenacity with which Confederate soldiers fought underscored their belief in the rights guaranteed by the Constitution. These attributes are the underpinning of our democratic society and represent the foundation on which this nation was built."[7]

Ta-Nehisi Coates, on the other hand, asserts that "the Confederate flag is directly tied to the Confederate cause, and the Confederate cause was white supremacy. This claim is not the result of revisionism. It does not require reading between the lines. It is the plain meaning of the words of those who bore the Confederate flag across history. These words must never be forgotten. Over the next few months the word 'heritage' will be repeatedly invoked. It would be derelict to not examine the exact contents of that heritage."[8]

As the 11 seceding states made their exits, their leaders imagined themselves as the legitimate heirs of the Founding Fathers of 1776. Like them, they sought to explain the reasons for their actions by issuing mini-Declarations of Independence known as "declarations of causes." In them, the seceding states make it very clear that they were declaring war on their country over the preservation of slavery. Mississippi's declaration asserted bluntly that their "position is thoroughly identified with the institution of slavery—the greatest material interest of the world ... a blow at slavery is a blow at commerce and civilization. That blow has been long aimed at the institution, and was at the point of reaching its consummation. There was no choice left us but submission to the mandates of abolition, or a dissolution of the Union, whose principles had been subverted to work out our ruin...." Georgia opened its declaration with the statement that "for the last ten years we have had numerous and serious causes of complaint against our non-slave-holding confederate States with reference to the subject of African slavery. They have endeavored to weaken our security, to disturb our domestic peace and tranquility, and persistently refused to comply with their express constitutional obligations to us in reference to that property...." South Carolina, like many of her sister states, objected at length to the refusal of Northern states to enforce the Fugitive Slave Act. Texas observed indignantly,

"In all the non-slave-holding States ... the people have formed themselves into a great sectional party ... based upon an unnatural feeling
of hostility to these Southern States and their beneficent and patri-
archal system of African slavery, proclaiming the debasing doctrine
of equality of all men, irrespective of race or color—a doctrine at
war with nature, in opposition to the experience of mankind, and in
violation of the plainest revelations of Divine Law. They demand the
abolition of negro slavery throughout the confederacy, the recognition of political equality between the white and negro races, and avow
their determination to press on their crusade against us, so long as a
negro slave remains in these States."[9]

Texas went on to clearly state its own certainty of white supremacy: "We hold as undeniable truths that the governments of the various States, and of the confederacy itself, were established exclusively
by the white race, for themselves and their posterity; that the African
race had no agency in their establishment; that they were rightfully
held and regarded as an inferior and dependent race, and in that condition only could their existence in this country be rendered beneficial
or tolerable." Nor was Texas alone in this assertion. Georgia wrote
that "the question of slavery was the great difficulty in the way of
the formation of the Constitution. While the subordination and the
political and social inequality of the African race was fully conceded
by all, it was plainly apparent that slavery would soon disappear from
what are now the non-slave-holding States of the original thirteen ..."
and says of the Republican party that "the prohibition of slavery in
the Territories, hostility to it everywhere, the equality of the black and
white races, disregard of all constitutional guarantees in its favor, were
boldly proclaimed by its leaders and applauded by its followers. With
these principles on their banners and these utterances on their lips
the majority of the people of the North demand that we shall receive
them as our rulers." Mississippi denounced the antislavery interest,
saying that it "advocates negro equality, socially and politically, and
promotes insurrection and incendiarism in our midst."

The Declarations of Cause do also include some references to
preserving liberty, as the SCV maintains. Georgia's words about
Northerners presenting themselves to the Southern states as rulers
have already been quoted. Mississippi wrote that "utter subjugation
awaits us in the Union, if we should consent longer to remain in it.

It is not a matter of choice, but of necessity. We must either sub-
mit to degradation, and to the loss of property worth four billions
of money, or we must secede from the Union framed by our fathers,
to secure this as well as every other species of property." Many declarations of cause asserted that the federal government had usurped
excessive powers and failed to respect the sovereignty of states. But
the documents also made it abundantly clear that the freedom sought
after was specifically the freedom to own slaves; the declarations of
cause denounced those Northern states that had declined to enforce
the Fugitive Slave Act in spite of the federal government's supporting it. The documents also make it abundantly clear that the liberty
they seek is specifically the liberty to enslave black people, who are
very frequently (as in the case above) described not as humans but as
"property." Texas stated that "in this free government all white men
are and of right ought to be entitled to equal civil and political rights."
The same declaration complained bitterly that the government had
not sufficiently helped Texans in fighting off "Indian savages" and
"murderous banditti" from Mexico—that is, the original inhabitants
of the land they had taken by force. Presumably the Confederate
leaders of Texas believed that those people also were not entitled to
rights, because they were not white. The language used to describe
them suggested that they may not even be people at all. If one accepts
this narrowed definition of the human race, it is possible to accept
that the South seceded over "liberty." But once people who are not
white are admitted to be human, this claim becomes untenable.

One caveat is in order. The documents above provide a clear and
ugly summary of why the Confederacy was originally established.
This is completely separate from the question of why any individual
Confederate soldier may have chosen to fight. Once war was declared
and imminent, it's wholly probable that individuals who weren't particularly pro-slavery joined up in hopes of protecting their homes and
families from a hostile army, or in the blind fervor that war in its
early stages tends to evoke, or in fear of what their neighbors would
do to them if they were seen as traitors. These people, as well as those
who joined for clearly pro-slavery and white-supremacist reasons, did
in many cases fight bravely and suffer greatly. Many of their civilian
relatives also suffered in the war's later stages. There were atrocities
committed by the Northern army. There is no need or excuse to claim

that all those who fought for the South were villains, still less that all those who fought for the North were heroes.

But this individual complexity does not mitigate the raw evil of the cause for which the Confederacy fought, nor should it change how we use its symbols now. Under the Third Reich there were doubtless German soldiers who took up arms, not out of anti-Semitism, but out of vague patriotic loyalty or out of fear of what the government would do to them if they refused. Many of them fought bravely. Many of them and their civilian kin suffered greatly in the end stages and the aftermath of the war. There were atrocities committed by Allied as well as Axis troops. There is no need or excuse to claim that all those who fought for the Reich were villains, still less that all who fought for the Allies were heroes. Nevertheless, the army of the Reich is not now glorified in the country it once claimed to defend, and the symbols under which it fought are now understood to be symbols of hate. Consider Georgetown Law professor Paul Butler's retort, just days after the Charleston massacre, to a UDC representative defending the battle flag because it "honored her [White] ancestors of whom she was proud":[10]

> I have no respect for your ancestors. As far as your ancestors are concerned, I shouldn't be a law professor at Georgetown. I should be a slave. That's why they fought that war. I don't understand what it means to be proud of a legacy of terrorism and violence. Last week at this time, I was in Israel. The idea that a German would say, you know, that thing we did called the Holocaust was wrong, but I respect the courage of my Nazi ancestors. That wouldn't happen. The reason that people can say what you said in the United States is because, again, Black life doesn't matter to a lot of people.

Reconstruction—And Its Discontents

For a brief time—all too brief—after the Civil War there was some attempt to undercut white supremacy and extend the privileges of citizenship to black Americans. This was often equivocal. Most land was given, not to the former slaves who had worked it, but to the slave masters or their descendants, or in some cases to Northern whites. This left black people as dependent laborers; under President Andrew

Johnson, who had assured his listeners in an 1864 speech (before he was president, of course) that they had a "white man's government,"[11] the Southern states were allowed to pass "black codes" that severely restricted their rights. Mississippi, for instance, forbade freedmen from leasing or renting land and required them to work for white landowners under labor contracts and to be imprisoned if they broke those contracts.[12] Johnson's chosen provisional governor for Florida explained to freed black people that they "must not think because you are as free as white people you are their equal, because you are not."[13]

But Johnson's policies alarmed and angered many, and under his successor President Grant, the Southern states were required to ratify the Thirteenth Amendment to the Constitution, ending slavery and involuntary servitude; the Fourteenth Amendment, declaring all persons born or naturalized in the US to be citizens; and the Fifteenth, guaranteeing the right to vote to all citizens irrespective of "race, color, or previous condition of servitude." Given the bare chance of equality before the law, black Southerners began to vote, and to run for office, and to gain seats in Southern state legislatures, even taking the majority of the lower house of the South Carolina legislature. Two black Senators and twenty black Congressmen were elected to the US Congress.

This progress was fiercely resented by white supremacists. Sometimes the backlash took legal form: the Georgia legislature voted to expel all its black members in 1868. Sometimes it came out in propaganda: one example is Columbia University scholar John Burgess's description of Reconstruction: "In place of government by the most intelligent and virtuous part of the people for the benefit of the governed, here was government by the most ignorant and vicious part of the population.... A black skin means membership in a race of men which has never of itself succeeded in subjecting passion to reason; has never, therefore, created civilization of any kind."[14] Sometimes it came out in domestic terrorism, both covert and overt. In Meridian, Mississippi, shortly before the 1872 election (when Grant was running for a second term) white Democrats, including many former Confederates and some five hundred men in Klan gear, marched repeatedly in the streets. When some black citizens formed up as a militia and got into an altercation with some of the white militants, the black leader was arrested; so were the black leaders of a church meeting that called for peace. A firefight broke out at their trial—there were conflicting accounts of how that started—and three of the black defendants were killed.[15] This was not an isolated incident (in the North or the South), and the violence grew worse as the federal troops who were supposed to monitor elections were drawn off to fight against the Indians in the West. Egerton further notes that "the concomitant spike in white vigilantism marked the beginning of the end of Reconstruction in much of the former Confederacy."[16] In 1877, when the presidential election between Democrat Samuel Tilden and Republican Rutherford B. Hayes depended on the contested electoral-college votes of three Southern states, Hayes won support by promising the full withdrawal of Union troops.[17] Egerton quotes Congressman Robert Smalls as saying that "by the time he left office in March 1887 ... fifty-three thousand African Americans had been murdered, mostly in the South, in the years since emancipation."[18]

In 1890 the Mississippi state legislature amended the state constitution, imposing poll taxes and literacy tests that were used to effectively disenfranchise black voters.[19] In 1894 the Mississippi state flag was redesigned to include the Confederate battle flag. In 1896 the US Supreme Court ruled in *Plessy v. Ferguson* that segregation, under the guise of "separate but equal" facilities, was constitutional. By 1900 the other Southern states had followed Mississippi's lead in restricting the franchise, and a *New York Times* editorial observed that "Northern men ... no longer denounce the suppression of the Negro vote.... The necessity of it under the supreme law of self-preservation is candidly recognized."[20] The erection of Confederate monuments on courthouse grounds and in other public places across the Southern states peaked in the following 10 years.[21] (There was a second, smaller spike during the civil rights era discussed in the next section.)

Considering this history in light of Sartrian "bad faith" yields paradoxical results. Historical scholarship of the past several decades has established that the white-supremacist views reflected in the secession declarations were commonplace among antebellum whites, including many abolitionists who also favored racial separation. The Supreme Court itself, by a 7–2 vote in 1857, enshrined in American constitutional law the principle that black people "are not included, and were not intended to be included, under the word 'citizens' in the Constitution, and can therefore claim none of the rights and privileges which that instrument provides for and secures to citizens of the United States. On the contrary, they were at that time [of America's founding] considered as a subordinate and inferior class of beings who had been subjugated by the dominant race, and, whether emancipated or not, yet remained subject to their authority, and had no rights or privileges but such as those who held the power and the Government might choose to grant them."[22] Thus, although the Republican Party of 1860 opposed the expansion of slavery into new territories, it specifically stated its opposition to its abolition where it already existed and proposed neither political nor civil racial equality. The secessionists of 1860, then, based their arguments and appeals on longstanding, majoritarian, and utterly racist views of black people as a permanently inferior race. Furthermore, they denied any contradiction between these views and the sweeping egalitarian ideals of 1776 by pointing out the many laws sharply limiting the rights of free blacks in non-slave states.

Certainly the secessionists were not cynics in the Sartrian sense: they believed every racist word they said or wrote. Whether they were acting in good faith or bad faith is a trickier matter. The fact that such racism was the hegemonic national discourse makes the secessionists' good faith more likely, since they didn't have to "convince themselves" of anything other than what most [white] people already believed.

Civil Rights and "Massive Resistance"

In the aftermath of World War II, the defeat of the Nazi regime clearly revealed the atrocities that regime had committed, white America began to look uneasily at its own white supremacist tendencies. Hitler, after all, had admired American writings and policies related to eugenics and had written in *Mein Kampf* that "there is today one state in which at least weak beginnings toward a better conception [of citizenship] are noticeable. Of course, it is not our model German Republic, but the United States...."[23]

Black Americans were way ahead of them. In 1947, buoyed by successes during World War II, labor and civil rights leader A. Philip Randolph renewed efforts to end discrimination in the armed services, urging blacks to resist if Congress passed President Truman's requested peacetime draft.

For this or other reasons, the federal government made some moves toward considering the rights of its black citizens. At its 1948 convention the Democratic Party, which for decades had commanded the votes of former Confederates wholly unwilling to vote for the party of Lincoln, adopted the following language after hours of bitter debate:

> The Democratic Party commits itself to continuing its efforts to eradi-
> cate all racial, religious and economic discrimination.
>
> We again state our belief that racial and religious minorities must
> have the right to live, the right to work, the right to vote, the full and
> equal protection of the laws, on a basis of equality with all citizens as
> guaranteed by the Constitution.
>
> We highly commend President Harry S. Truman for his coura-
> geous stand on the issue of civil rights.
>
> We call upon the Congress to support our President in guarantee-
> ing these basic and fundamental American Principles: (1) the right of
> full and equal political participation; (2) the right to equal opportunity
> of employment; (3) the right of security of person; (4) and the right of
> equal treatment in the service and defense of our nation.[24]

The language about "security of person" referred in part to declaring lynching a federal crime.

Delegates from Alabama and Mississippi stormed out of the convention in response to this language and joined together with other Southern Democrats to establish a splinter party, formally known as the States' Rights Democratic Party but better remembered today as the Dixiecrats. Vulnerable to re-election defeat and needing votes from the growing black electorate in northern states, Truman eventually moved left on race. On 26 July 1948—only two weeks after the Dixiecrats exited the convention—Truman signed Executive Order 9981 abolishing racial segregation in the armed forces.

At their convention in Alabama, the Dixiecrats nominated South Carolina governor Strom Thurmond as their presidential candidate and added language to their platform explaining their objections to the civil-rights proposals of their fellow Democrats:

We stand for the segregation of the races and the racial integrity of each race; the constitutional right to choose one's associates; to accept private employment without governmental interference, and to earn one's living in any lawful way. We oppose the elimination of segregation, the repeal of miscegenation statutes, the control of private employment by Federal bureaucrats called for by the misnamed civil rights program. We favor home-rule, local self-government and a minimum interference with individual rights.

We oppose and condemn the action of the Democratic Convention in sponsoring a civil rights program calling for the elimination of segregation, social equality by Federal fiat, regulations of private employment practices, voting, and local law enforcement.

... We unreservedly condemn the effort to establish in the United States a police nation that would destroy the last vestige of liberty enjoyed by a citizen.[25]

Here, as in the Confederate declarations of secession, there is an appeal to liberty and individual rights that can be understood only as limited exclusively to whites. The enforcement of anti-discrimination statutes in hiring and voter registration is seen as creating "a police nation" and interfering with "individual rights." The forbidding of interracial marriage, the disenfranchisement of black voters, and the enforcement of segregation statutes are not. This makes sense only if black people are not seen as fully human, if one accepts that black lives and liberties do not matter.

This peculiar and limited version of "liberty" was again proclaimed in the presence of a Confederate flag: of today's familiar Confederate flag, the rectangular version of the battle flag, which was waved by enthusiastic Dixiecrat delegates.[26]

The Dixiecrats succeeded in getting their candidate on the ballot as the Democratic nominee in Alabama, Mississippi, Louisiana, and South Carolina. Thurman carried those states, but not Georgia, which had listed him as a third-party candidate, or any state outside the Deep South; it was noted that Thurman performed best in areas with the highest black populations, presumably because white interest in black voter disenfranchisement was highest there.[27]

While the Dixiecrats failed on the national level, their views—and the flag associated with them—remained prominent in several

Southern states. After the Supreme Court called for desegregation in its 1954 decision *Brown v. Board of Education*, prominent politicians in former Confederate states declared that their rights were again being trampled by the federal government. A political pressure group calling itself "The Defenders of State Sovereignty and Individual Liberties" (that word liberty again!) organized in late 1954 to preserve school segregation in Virginia. Virginia Senator Harry Byrd called for "massive resistance" to desegregation in 1956, and Virginia governor Thomas B. Stanley established an all-white commission to make suggestions about the state response to *Brown v. Board*. They proposed measures for preserving segregation based on local district initiatives. The governor decided instead that the state itself should block the assignment of black pupils to white schools and close any school whose desegregation was mandated, should take various technical legal steps to make it more difficult for the NAACP to file civil-rights lawsuits,[28] and should create the "Commission on Constitutional Government" to whip up opposition to desegregation. The *Encyclopedia Virginia* notes, "With Confederate flags waving in the galleries, the legislators passed the Massive Resistance plan."[29]

Also in 1956, Georgia incorporated the ANV Confederate flag into its state flag. The Georgia State Senate Research Office is quite clear about the motives behind this change, while trying to dissociate these from other flag uses that they saw as legitimate:

> Despite some nonracist uses, the Dixiecrat, segregationist, and Klan uses of the flag by that time had distorted the flag's connection with the Confederate nation and its soldiers. The raising of the battle flag over the capitols is clear—intimidation of those who would enforce integration and a statement of firm resolve to resist integration....
> When the battle flag was incorporated into the Georgia state flag, the state was in a desperate situation to preserve segregation. Resisting, avoiding, undermining, and circumventing integration was the 1956 General Assembly's primary objective. The adoption of the battle flag was an integral, albeit small, part of this resistance. The 1956 state flag, as Representative Denmark Groover so clearly stated, "will serve notice that we intend to uphold what we stood for, will stand for, and will fight for."

Elsewhere they say, "The lawmakers came to Atlanta clearly with the intention of giving swift and overwhelming approval to a series of segregation bills designed to prevent race-mixing in classrooms, public parks, golf courses, playgrounds, and swimming pools," and note that Speaker of the House Marvin Moate said in his opening address to the House's 1956 session that "certain problems exist that are peculiar to our section [of the nation] and with which the other parts of our country have little knowledge and a complete lack of understanding.... Not since the days of the carpetbagger and the days of Reconstruction have problems more vital to the welfare of all our people confronted the General Assembly." One may surmise that "our people" were here understood to be whites.[30]

Finally, they point out that the change to the flag was opposed by various groups set up to memorialize Confederate veterans, including the United Daughters of the Confederacy, the Ladies Memorial Association, and the John B. Gordon Camp of the Sons of Confederate Veterans. "Given the role that these organizations play in memorializing and paying tribute to the Confederacy," the authors say, "they clearly would have lent their support to the sponsors of the new flag if they believed that it truly paid tribute to Confederate veterans."[31]

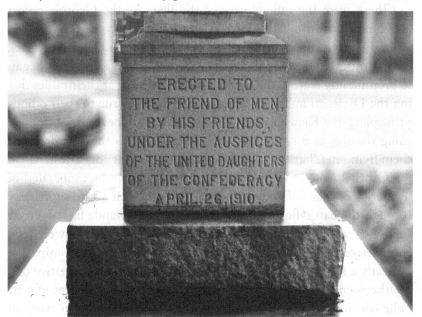

United Daughters of the Confederacy Monument, Willis Park, Bainbridge, Georgia.

Governor George Wallace of Alabama similarly invoked the Confederacy in opposing desegregation, both through his rhetoric and through his use of the flag. In his 1963 inaugural address he said, "Today I have stood, where once Jefferson Davis stood, and took [sic] an oath to my people. It is very appropriate then that from this Cradle of the Confederacy, this very Heart of the Great Anglo-Saxon Southland, that today we sound the drum for freedom as have our generations of forebears before us done, time and again through history. Let us rise to the call of the freedom-loving blood that is in us and send our answer to the tyranny that clanks its chains upon the South. In the name of the greatest people that have ever trod this earth, I draw the line in the dust and toss the gauntlet before the feet of tyranny ... and I say ... segregation now ... segregation tomorrow ... segregation forever."[32] Seemingly he heard nothing ironic in describing attempts to protect black liberties as "clanking chains," or describing the pro-slavery cause as a valiant defense of freedom. And when pro–civil-rights Attorney General Robert Kennedy came to the Capitol to meet Governor Wallace in April 1963, Wallace raised the Confederate Naval Jack over the Capitol and didn't take it down again until Kennedy was gone.[33]

These were the official uses of the flag. As the Georgia report above notes, it also had illicit connections, hardly more racist but more directly violent. The Ku Klux Klan had been terrorizing black communities since soon after the end of the Civil War, but they began to prominently feature the Confederate battle flag at their rallies during the Dixiecrat and pro-segregation period.[34] True to their odious "principles," the Klan and its fellow travelers have never since stopped using the flag as a symbol of white supremacy, as the abundance of them flying in Charlottesville, Virginia, in August 2017 attests.[35]

On this issue at least, the Klan and its ilk can be exonerated of hypocrisy or bad faith: they openly proclaim their white supremacy through the battle flag. As law professor Neil Gotanda has observed, such uses made the flag an undeniable symbol of white power: "The confederate flag is a complex symbol, but whiteness as domination is clearly a significant aspect of its symbolism. As representative of a Southern culture, the Confederate flag has provided a point of symbolic controversy as it flies over Southern statehouses or is worn in schools or displayed in public."[36]

But exoneration cannot be granted to the politicians and commentators who have, over the past 70 years, defended the battle flag and those who fly it by ignoring or eliding the well-known history set forth above. That history demonstrates that from its Civil War origins through its Dixiecrat revival and right down to the present day, the Confederate battle flag has been and is inextricably interwoven with white supremacy. How they manage to ignore that history and engage in that bad faith is the subject of the next chapter.

Notes

1   John M. Coski, "Embattled Banner: The True History of the Confederate Flag," https://www.historynet.com/embattled-banner-the-convoluted-history-of-the-confederate-flag.htm.

2   The use of the term "subaltern" comes from Gayatri Spivak's essay "Can the Subaltern Speak?," which is a foundational piece of work in postcolonial and postmodern studies. She coins the use of subaltern from her work on Antonio Gramsci's Marxist critique of cultural hegemony. Gayatri Spivak, "Can the Subaltern Speak?," in Cary Nelson and Lawrence Grossberg, eds., *Marxism and the Interpretation of Culture* (London: Macmillan, 1988), 271–315.

3   In 1933 Arnautoff painted one of the famous Coit Tower murals, which were subjected to right-wing political censorship even as they were being created. Adam Brinklow, "85 Fascinating Facts about Coit Tower for Its 85th Birthday," *Curbed San Francisco*, 8 October 2018.

4   Robert W. Cherny, "'No Proven Communist Should Hold a Position at Stanford': Victor Mikhail Arnautoff, the House Un-American Activities Committee, and Stanford," *Sandstone & Tile* 37.3 (2013): 6–7.

5   Robert W. Cherny, *Victor Arnautoff and the Politics of Art* (Urbana: University of Illinois Press, 2017), 110.

6   B. Davis, "This Artist Painted the Black Radical Response to the George Washington Slaveholder Murals. Here's Why He Stands against Destroying Them," *Artnet News*, 10 July 2019.

7   *Sons of Confederate Veterans* homepage, http://www.scv.org/new/.

8   T.N. Coates, "What This Cruel War Was Over," *The Atlantic*, 22 June 2015.

9   All quotations are taken from the primary source collection *The Declaration of Causes of Seceding States* on the website of the American Battlefield Trust, https://www.battlefields.org/learn/primary-sources/declaration-causes-seceding-states.

10   Robert Fikes Jr., "Pride, Prejudice, and the Confederate Flag," *Pittsburgh Courier*, 3 July 2015.

11   Douglas R. Egerton, *The Wars of Reconstruction: The Brief, Violent History of America's Most Progressive Era* (London: Bloomsbury Press, 2014), 173.

12   Howard Zinn, *A People's History of the United States* (New York: HarperCollins, 2003).

13   Egerton, *The Wars of Reconstruction*, 174.

14   Quoted in Zinn, *People's History*, 202.

15   Egerton, *The Wars of Reconstruction*, 284–86.

16   Ibid., 287.

17   C. Vann Woodward, *Reunion and Reaction: The Compromise of 1877 and the End of Reconstruction* (Boston: Little, Brown & Co., 1966).

18   Egerton, *The Wars of Reconstruction*, 287.

19   "This Day in History, Nov. 1, 1980: Mississippi Constitution," *Zinn Education Project*, https://www.zinnedproject.org/news/tdih/mississippi-constitution/.

20   Quoted in Zinn, *People's History*, 207.

21   See graph in the 2016 "Whose Heritage?" report by the Southern Poverty Law Center, https://www.splcenter.org/sites/default/files/com_whose_heritage.pdf, 14.

22   *Scott v. Sandford*, 60 U.S. 393 (1857), 405.

23   Quoted in Lisa Ko, "Unwanted Sterilization and Eugenics Programs in the United States," *PBS*, 29 January 2016.

24   "1948 Democratic Party Platform," archived on the website of the American Presidency Project of the University of California at Santa Barbara, www.presidency.ucsb.edu/documents/republican-party-platform-1948.

25   "Platform of the States Rights Democratic Party," archived on the website of the American Presidency Project of the University of California at Santa Barbara, www.presidency.ucsb.edu/documents/1948-democratic-party-platform.

26   See image from the convention at John M. Coski's "Embattled Banner: The Convoluted History of the Confederate Flag," https://www.historynet.com/embattled-banner-the-convoluted-history-of-the-confederate-flag.htm. See also the assertion in the text of Frances Stead Sellers, "The Confederate Flag: A 150-year Battle," *Washington Post*, 23 October 2018.

27   Scott E. Buchanan, "Dixiecrats," *New Georgia Encyclopedia*, https://www.georgiaencyclopedia.org/articles/government-politics/dixiecrats.

28   Brian J. Daugherity, "Desegregation in Public Schools," *Encyclopedia Virginia*, https://www.encyclopediavirginia.org/Desegregation_in_Public_Schools.

29   James H. Hershman Jr., "Massive Resistance," *Encyclopedia Virginia*, https://www.encyclopediavirginia.org/Massive_Resistance.

30   Alexander J. Azarian and Eden Fesshazion, "The State Flag of Georgia: The 1956 Change in Its Historical Context," Georgia State Senate Research Office, www.senate.ga.gov/sro/Documents/StudyCommRpts/00StateFlag.pdf.

31   Ibid.

32   "Inaugural address of Governor George Wallace, which was delivered at the Capitol in Montgomery, Alabama," Alabama Department of Archives and History, http://digital.archives.alabama.gov/cdm/singleitem/collection/voices/id/2952/rec/5.

33   WSFA 12 News Staff and Morgan Carlson, "History of the Confederate flag on Alabama Capitol Grounds," *WSFA 12 News*, 22 June 2015.

34   N. Shavin, "The Confederate Flag Is a Racist Symbol: Just Ask the KKK," *New Republic*, 1 July 2015; O. Ortman, "Finding Meaning in the Confederate Flag: The KKK Era," *Gettysburg Compiler*, 19 September 2018.

35   Doug Mataconis, "Charlottesville Reopens the Debate over Confederate Symbols," *Outside the Beltway*, 15 August 2017, https://www.outsidethebeltway.com/charlottesville-reopens-the-debate-over-confederate-symbols/.

36   Neil Gotanda, "A Critique of 'Our Constitution Is Color-Blind,'" *Stanford Law Review* 44 (November 1991): 62.

Chapter Seven

THE FLAG TODAY

Pride, Heritage, Terror, Freedom

The Confederate Flag in the US Military

TODAY THE ARGUMENT ABOUT WHAT THE CONFEDERATE battle flag represents continues to inflame the so-called "culture wars," as overt racists claim the flag as a symbol of white supremacy and others resist those claims with arguments that the flag represents honor, heritage, liberty, and other "American" values. Given the fact that these arguments ignore far more history than they cite, this latter group could fairly be characterized as covert racists who rely on bad-faith arguments to advance their views.

Some Confederate enthusiasts point to the flag's use by Southern troops in the US army in later wars as a sign that it simply indicates valor and regional pride. The Confederate flag was flown before President Wilson in 1916 as a group of Southern soldiers proclaimed their willingness to fight in World War I.[1] (Segregation among federal employees had spread under Wilson's administration, and apparently with his consent; when civil rights leader William Monroe Trotter protested this in 1914, Wilson sent him away unceremoniously while he was still trying to speak.[2]) The first flag flown over the captured Shuri Castle in Okinawa as World War II ended was the rebel flag.[3] During the Korean War—after President Truman integrated the military—the NAACP noted that sales of the Confederate flag quadrupled, and many were requested by soldiers overseas; they expressed the hope that this was an empty fad.

A Confederate battle flag in rural Randolph County, North Carolina.

But by the time of the Vietnam War there were some concerns that soldiers might be flying that flag as white supremacists, not simply as valiant Southerners. Greg Grandin reports on one incident in *The Nation*: "'We are fighting and dying in a war that is not very popular in the first place,' Lieutenant Eddie Kitchen, a 33-year-old African-American stationed in Vietnam, wrote to his mother in Chicago in late February 1968, 'and we still have some people who are still fighting the Civil War.' Kitchen ... reported a rapid proliferation of Confederate flags, mounted on jeeps and flying over some bases. 'The Negroes here are afraid and cannot do anything,' Kitchen added.

Two weeks later he was dead, officially listed as 'killed in action.' His mother believed that he had been murdered by white soldiers in retaliation for objecting to the flag."[4] When Lt. William Calley was tried for war crimes as a result of the My Lai massacre, ardent segregationist governor George Wallace visited Calley in the stockade, asked the president to pardon him, and spoke favorably of him at a rally replete with Confederate flags; both pro-[5] and anti-[6]Confederate sources saw parallels—of different sorts—between the Vietnam War and the Civil War. The Confederate flag appeared again in Iraq, and in the tent of a platoon which later became notorious for torturing (non-white) prisoners.[7]

It could fairly be pointed out that Calley and the Afghan interrogators committed their atrocities under the US flag and that it is very difficult to find any national symbol that has not been used in conjunction with atrocities. It is also true that most nations have a longer history than the Confederacy and a more complex record on matters of race.

Heritage and Remembrance

Some groups claim persistently that the flag represents "heritage, not hate," and describe it as an apolitical symbol of remembrance. The United Daughters of the Confederacy, who broadly opposed the incorporation of the battle flag into the Georgia flag, now take this line. Their home page begins with an acknowledgment of the controversy over Confederate symbols. They state that the UDC is "grieved that certain hate groups have taken the Confederate flag and other symbols as their own," "totally denounces any individual or group that promotes racial divisiveness or white supremacy," call on such people to stop using Confederate symbols for their "abhorrent and reprehensible purposes," express sorrow at the fact that some people find anything connected with the Confederacy to be reprehensible, point out that Confederates were Americans, and go on to say that the UDC does not judge them or "impose the standards of the 21st century on these Americans of the 19th century." They appeal to be allowed to honor the memory of their ancestors, say that all Americans should honor their ancestors and that such diversity makes us stronger, and ask all Americans to join them in affirming that "Confederate monuments and statues are part of our shared American history and should remain in place."[8] While acknowledging and denouncing the work of known hate groups, the UDC ignores the legal and "respectable" support for segregation and discrimination that have long been associated with Confederate symbols. It also seems to raise the question of why the long rich history of the American South should be best remembered by using the symbols of a very short-lived "nation" brought into existence, as we saw above, specifically to defend slavery and white supremacy.

The Sons of Confederate Veterans, the UDC's male counterpart, take a more truculent line. Their homepage opens with their charge from 1906: "To you, Sons of Confederate Veterans, we will commit the vindication of the cause for which we fought. To your strength will be given the defense of the Confederate soldier's good name, the guardianship of his history, the emulation of his virtues, the perpetuation of those principles which he loved and which you love also, and those ideals which made him glorious and which you also cherish."[9] They don't specify just what those principles and ideals might be, but they go on, as quoted above, to assert that "the preservation of liberty and freedom was the motivating factor in the South's decision to fight the Second American Revolution. The tenacity with which Confederate soldiers fought underscored their belief in the rights guaranteed by the Constitution. These attributes are the underpinning of our democratic society and represent the foundation on which this nation was built." This tone of veneration for the Confederates and the Confederacy permeates the site. New Orleans mayor Mitch Landrieu, who called for the removal of Confederate monuments in the public square, noted, "There is a difference between remembrance of history and reverence of it."[10] Reverence for the Confederacy raises some troubling questions.

While the UDC points out its devotion to quiet good works, the SCV is clearly politically active. Their blog and their Heritage Defense page describe their insistence on the retention of Confederate monuments in the public square and on the display of the Confederate flag on license plates and in other forms at NASCAR races and other events. Their leader also declared (in 2017, at which point it seems the blog stopped being updated) "to the Confederacy" a Law

Enforcement Appreciation Day on which to push back against the "current vicious and despicable attacks being waged against the law enforcement officers around the country today," praised their valor and sacrifice, and expounded on the moral duty of all citizens to support them.[11] What, one might wonder, does support for a group of rebels who attempted to overthrow the US government have to do with support for the armed agents of that government? The context of the Black Lives Matter movement may suggest a race-based common thread.

The SCV's official Facebook page,[12] which is still, unlike the blog, being updated, continues to announce events in defense/celebration of Confederate monuments. Their other causes cast an interesting sidelight on how they may interpret the principles and values they are charged with protecting. They tout sales of "Make Dixie Great Again" caps (yes, closely resembling MAGA hats), tributes to their heroes George Washington and Jefferson Davis, criticisms of Lincoln, and a recent article condemning protestors who shouted and waved signs at one of their events for lawmakers: "These violent and extreme members of the mob will not stop their efforts with the eradication of Confederate heritage. Their aim is to destroy every contribution and legacy throughout our history that stands as proof that their desired outcome for our country is a bad idea. Their end game is to literally destroy us, the people.... Everything we do is to honor our ancestors. We are doing nothing wrong and have nothing to apologize for. It is an anomaly in human history that anyone should be denied this basic right, especially when those being honored are responsible for so much of what we enjoy today."[13] They don't explain which of our present enjoyments are due to the Confederacy. Nor do they explain how one would tell the difference between "we the people" and "the mob."

Jefferson Beauregard Sessions, III

The life and career of Jefferson Beauregard Sessions III provides an excellent case study of someone engaging in bad-faith ignorance in defending the battle flag and discussing race. He was born just 18 months before the Dixiecrat schism, and Sessions's life of continuous white privilege has paralleled the nation's twisting path on race, racism, and the battle flag. He was also the first Senator to endorse Donald Trump for president, at a time when many Republican leaders were denouncing him for racist comments.[14]

Born in Selma, Alabama, on 24 December 1946, to business owner Jefferson B. Sessions, Jr., and the former Abbie Powe, Sessions grew up near tiny Hybart, Alabama, in Wilcox County. Located in the "black belt," Wilcox was the state's poorest county, a place where not a single African American was registered to vote, despite constituting 77.9 per cent of the population.[15]

According to a 1965 desegregation lawsuit, Jim Crow shaped Wilcox's separate but unequal school system.[16] In fact, Wilcox provided a quality education to white students like Sessions because of segregation, spending five times more per white pupil than per black pupil, while black schools lacked central heat, indoor plumbing, regular maintenance, or up-to-date instructional materials, all of which white schools, like Wilcox Central High School, had. Sessions graduated from Wilcox Central in 1965.

Growing up in a pro-segregation household during the civil rights movement, Sessions was at the impressionable age of 16 when Alabama governor George Wallace pledged "segregation now, segregation tomorrow, segregation forever" in 1963, and 18 when the civil rights movement came to Wilcox in the form of voter-registration drives and the case against the school system.[17] Dr. Martin Luther King Jr. visited Wilcox County several times to assist in the fight. White resisters beat and killed civil rights activists and even led an armed assault on a leading black church in the summer of 1965.[18] Sessions was living in Wilcox for all of this; whether he participated or not, he certainly knew all about what was happening.

Also in 1965, Sessions decided to attend Huntingdon College in Montgomery, a private school for whites only, earning a BA in 1969.[19] He left the Democratic Party and was active in the Young Republicans at a time when only a small number of Southern whites were just beginning to switch to the GOP in response to Democratic support for civil rights. Sessions attended the University of Alabama School of Law, which in 1969 finally admitted its first black student, and graduated in 1973.

After serving five years as a US Attorney in Alabama, Sessions was nominated in 1986 for a federal judgeship by President Ronald

Reagan, yet he failed to persuade the Senate Judiciary Committee to send his nomination to the floor for a vote because of credible allegations of racist statements and behavior.[20] According to sworn testimony, while he was a US Attorney, Sessions called a black lawyer who worked for him "boy" and cautioned him to "be careful what you say to white folks." Sessions also called the ACLU and NAACP "un-American" and "Communist-inspired" because they "forced civil rights down the throats of people," but the KKK was "OK, until he learned that they smoked marijuana." Sessions denied using the term "boy" and being a racist, and defended the other comments.[21]

Jeff Sessions grew up in a racist household in a black-belt county where blacks did not vote, he directly benefited from school segregation, and while on the cusp of adulthood he witnessed the civil rights movement, including Dr. King himself, bringing the fight against white supremacy into his home county. He chose to attend a whites-only college, became active in the Republican party when the only white Southerners doing so were motivated by racism, was credibly accused of racist conduct by multiple witnesses, and has consistently opposed civil rights legislation and enforcement during his decades-long political career. All this time, pro-segregationists were constantly using the battle flag in their marches and demonstrations.

Yet in 2015, Sessions told an interviewer from a Birmingham, Alabama, radio station that the Confederate battle flag "is a huge part of who *we are* and the left is continually seeking, in a host of different ways, ... to delegitimize the fabulous accomplishments of *our country*."[22] In this statement about the Confederate flag, "our country" can mean only the Confederacy, and "we" must mean white people, but what were these so-called "fabulous accomplishments," given the utter failure of secession and the near destruction of the South in its wake?

Despite the barely covert racism of this statement, Sessions lacks the integrity of the Klan, for he immediately pivoted to faux concern over racist uses of the flag, admitting that "a lot [of] our good citizens feel like [the flag] was kind of commandeered" to support the "idea of anti-civil rights," and claiming that he was "sensitive" to that perspective.[23] Given his full-throated defense of the flag, it is hard to see how Sessions's alleged "sensitivity" has actually affected his conduct around this issue.

But the deeper issue is Sessions's bad faith. Growing up where and how he did, during a time when the battle flag was being used on a continuous basis by pro-segregationists, and only by them, Sessions has always been personally aware that the flag's predominant use has been as a symbol of "anti-civil rights" activism. His radical under-statement of what "a lot [of] our good citizens feel" about the flag amounts to a denial of his own manifest personal knowledge, as though he did not know what we know he knows.

Jeff Sessions's comments on the battle flag represent an excel-lent example of what philosopher Charles Mills has dubbed an "epis-temology of ignorance." Epistemology is the branch of philosophy that deals with the nature, scope, and sources of knowledge: how and why do we know what we know? The epistemology of ignorance turns that question on its head to ask: how and why do we ignore what we ignore? As the editors of a recent anthology entitled *Race and Epistemologies of Ignorance* state, "the epistemology of ignorance is an examination of the complex phenomena of ignorance, which has as its aim identifying different forms of ignorance, examining how they are produced and sustained, and what role they play in knowl-edge practices," emphasizing that "sometimes these 'unknowledges' are consciously produced, while at other times they are unconsciously generated and supported."[24]

When it comes to social issues of political importance, the use and abuse of history is one of the primary means for creating igno-rance of what the powers that be want suppressed. As Mills argues,

> What makes such denial [of facts] possible, of course, is the manage-
> ment of memory.... But if we need to understand collective memory,
> we also need to understand collective amnesia. Indeed, they go
> together insofar as memory is necessarily selective—out of the infinite
> sequence of events, some trivial, some momentous, we extract what
> we see as the crucial ones and organize them into an overall narrative.
> Social memory is then inscribed in textbooks, generated and regener-
> ated in ceremonies and official holidays, concretized in statues, parks,
> and monuments.[25]

As far as the Confederate flag is concerned, Mills demonstrates that its use is part and parcel of a larger "historical forgetting": "the 'for-getting' takes the form of whitewashing the atrocities of slavery—the 'magnolia myth' of paternalistic white aristocrats and happy, singing darkies that dominated American textbooks as late as the 1950s—and minimizing the extent to which 'the peculiar institution' was not a sectional problem but shaped the national economy, polity, and psychology."[26] Sessions, then, a product of segregated white schools throughout his scholastic career, unconsciously absorbed the ignorance of race and racism they taught; and, as an adult, despite all that he saw and experienced, he has consciously maintained that epistemic ignorance even as he has never wavered from defending white privilege. This is also what W.E.B. Du Bois called "the deliberately educated ignorance of white schools."[27]

Pride and Resentment

Still, these official memorial groups are considerably milder than some other online groups that proclaim their pride in Confederate heritage. Facebook offers numerous Confederate-supporting groups, including Rally for the Confederate Flag and Confederate, which offer statements of Christian devotion, pledges of allegiance to the rebel flag, assertions that black freedmen under Reconstruction didn't know what voting meant and were used as pawns by cynical carpetbaggers, warnings about the PC plot against America and the imminent threat of socialism (said to have been introduced to America by Lincoln), vehement objections to the legal admission of refugees and immigrants (described as taking needed resources from brave veterans and real Americans), and denunciations of undocumented immigrants (described as gang or cartel members). A strong case can be made that this goes beyond remembering the dead to justifying their white supremacy and extending it into the present day.

A similar smorgasbord of concerns—appeals for the preservation of Confederate monuments, rants against socialism, denunciations of immigrants, lurid accounts of crimes by immigrants and liberals, denunciations of political correctness—can be found on the website of the Conservative Citizens Council, the group that billed itself as a rebirth of the earlier White Citizens Councils and is credited with radicalizing the Charlottesville murderer. They candidly bring all these issues back to the root of white supremacy:

We believe the United States is a European country and that Americans are part of the European people. We believe that the United States derives from and is an integral part of European civilization and the European people and that the American people and government should remain European in their composition and character. We therefore oppose the massive immigration of non-European and non-Western peoples into the United States that threatens to transform our nation into a non-European majority in our lifetime.... We also oppose all efforts to mix the races of mankind, to promote non-white races over the European-American people through so-called "affirmative action" and similar measures, to destroy or denigrate the European-American heritage, including the heritage of the Southern people, and to force the integration of the races.

They also state their belief in the extreme importance of property rights and their repudiation of "the 'imperial judiciary' in the US Supreme Court and the federal courts that has usurped more and more power to itself in the last century and has imposed on our country the most odious and harmful rulings"[28]—presumably including desegregation. They go on to declare, like the secessionists and Governor Wallace, their devotion to liberty—for white people, this is clearly implied—and to God—who apparently in their view cares only for white people.

Another common theme in many of these forums is support for Donald Trump. Trump's own statements on Confederate symbols, like his statements on everything else, have been contradictory. *Time* magazine notes that when he was still running for president in June 2015, Trump was asked whether the Confederate flag flying above the South Carolina state house needed to be taken down. "I think it probably does, and I think they should put it in the museum," he replied. "Let it go. Respect whatever it is you have to respect because it was a point in time, and put it in a museum. But I would take it down, yes."[29] But in 2017, once he had won his election, in the aftermath of the deadly white-supremacist violence that came out around a pro-Confederate–monument demonstration in Charlottesville, Trump tweeted, "Sad to see the history and culture of our great country being ripped apart with the removal of our beautiful statues and monuments. You can't change history, but you can learn from it. Robert

E Lee, Stonewall Jackson—who's next, Washington, Jefferson? So foolish! Also the beauty that is being taken out of our cities, towns and parks will be greatly missed and never able to be comparably replaced!"[30] And of course, Trump, with his remarks about Mexican rapists and sh**hole countries, his crusade against illegal immigration, and his rollback of attempts to reduce racial bias in policing, has a strong appeal to white nationalists.

This is sometimes even acknowledged by his supporters. A 2016 *New York Times* interview quotes South Carolina state representative Steven Moss, who voted to retain the flag, explaining why some Trump supporters were also Confederate flag-wavers or vice versa: "He said he thought that it might be part of a backlash of working white voters who suspect that people—in their minds, often minorities—are taking advantage of the federal welfare system.... A lot of these people who go to work every day are in the line at the grocery store, and over half the people are bringing out these cards to pay for the groceries, he said."[31] This, of course, overlooks the fact that most people on welfare are white, and it also raises the question of whether the stark racial wealth gap might have something to do with centuries of legal racial discrimination ... but these questions do not seem to occur to the Representative or those whose viewpoint he is representing.

The Flag Moves North

In recent years, Confederate symbols have also been picked up by Northerners who don't have any obvious heritage connection to the South. The past three years have included controversy over sales of Confederate flags at county fairs in Ohio and New York, displays of Confederate flags inside and outside schools in Michigan,[32] New York,[33] and Oregon,[34] among many others. The explanations given by the flag-flyers vary widely. A parent of a New York student suspended for refusing to stop displaying the flag explained, "The people against it think it stands for something racist, but it's really a symbol of wanting freedom." This view was also taken by some shoppers for Confederate merchandise at a New York fair: One "summed up the flag's appeal in one word: 'Defiance.'" Another, an "Army private flying the Confederate flag on his hat, two necklaces and a belt buckle, confirmed the theory. 'Plain and simple, a rebel,' he said. 'Tell me not to do something, I'm going to do it.'" But another shopper at the same fair offered explanations reminiscent of the miscellany of issues threaded together by race which appear on some pro-Confederate forums: "David Van Leuven, 20, a farmworker wearing a belt buckle with the Confederate and American flags, said that for him, the flag signified 'states that seceded for what they believe in.' He added, 'What the government does to people these days is horrible—we've got veterans who are homeless and illegal aliens coming here and getting free health care.'" What, one might wonder, is the common thread between celebrating bold rebels and excoriating people who cross borders without legal papers? The most obvious link would appear to be race.

In this sense, the battle flag can be understood as a performative symbol of a form of racist white identity. The battle flag, according to law professor Jody D. Armour, "is what language philosophers call a 'performative'—a form of symbolic communication that performs (hence its name) a social action, such as bonding individuals together."[35] Before the Civil War and even after, white Americans generally agreed on the inferiority of blacks and the need to discriminate against them. As such, the American flag could stand for whites as a symbol of both the nation and of white supremacy. But as the Dixiecrats showed, once white people split over this issue, white supremacists needed a more specific symbol to distinguish themselves and their white supremacy, and the modified battle flag filled the bill admirably, as Armour points out: "performatives don't simply say something, they do something, and in political communication the thing that bonding performatives such as flags, monuments, melodies, and street names do is unify and rally individuals; they create collective social actors and forge social identities."[36] In this case, the social identity is that of white supremacy.

Racism, of course, is not new in the North, and it cannot be reduced to a Southern import. At the end of the Civil War, 19 of the 24 Northern states forbade voting by black people.[37] Other forms of segregation, enforced by violence, were common in the North as well as in the South. In 1871 Frederick Douglass lamented the murder of a black activist who had helped to desegregate public transportation in his Northern city—"Shooting colored men in Philadelphia seems to be the order of the day ..."—and observed bitterly that white supremacists in the North as well as the south resorted to "murder and intimidation of voters."[38] Black families fleeing the South during the Great Migration of the early twentieth century found themselves restricted to certain neighborhoods for living and were regarded with suspicion and hostility by their white neighbors, as described in Isabel Wilkerson's book *The Warmth of Other Suns*.[39] And racist groups primarily associated with the Confederacy in the popular imagination have been in the North for some time. The Klan had an active membership among "respectable" people in Buffalo, New York, in the 1920s, capitalizing on fears of Others—in Buffalo's case, primarily Catholics and Germans.[40] In 2018 the Klan made its presence felt in New York again, leaving overtly white-supremacist recruitment fliers on cars or in bags with candy at the end of driveways where schoolkids waited for buses.[41] Many officials and ordinary people voiced concerns—while others defended the flyers as free speech, pointing out that such speech is protected even when deeply offensive.

It's true that much hateful speech is legally protected. It's also true that sometimes that speech leads to actual violence. And in recent years that violence has sometimes been connected with Confederate symbols. In 2015 a group of Confederate-flag enthusiasts in Georgia were indicted on terrorism charges for driving into a black neighborhood with Confederate flags flying, stopping outside a home where a child's birthday was in progress and yelling threats and racial slurs at party guests.[42] The driver of one of the flag-bearing trucks said he was just defending himself against attack by the black people, but the courts didn't agree. In 2017 two of the flag enthusiasts were sentenced to 6 to 13 years in prison for assault as well as terrorism-related charges; other group members had already pled guilty and accepted lighter sentences.[43] In this case the damage stopped at threats. Sometimes, of course, it doesn't stop there; no one will soon forget the church massacre in Charleston, or the shouting of Nazi slogans around Confederate memorials, the beating of counter-demonstrators, or the murder of Heather Heyer in Charlottesville.

No one will soon forget—but just what will they remember? After the Charlottesville massacre many institutions grappled with the meaning of their Confederate flags and monuments, and some actually removed them. But the Klan also rallied to defend the flag after the Charlottesville massacre—and after Charleston, and after

Charlottesville the sale of Confederate flags climbed sharply.[44] A piece in the conservative *Washington Times* argues that white people buy Confederate flags to assert their First Amendment freedoms, and also because they are angry at being told they are racist.[45]

My first response is exasperation: What would it take to convince people that the "freedom" to promote the enslavement or subjugation of others is not a human right? My second is some degree of sympathy for those who do not wish to accept that their cherished symbols are defined by the worst outrages committed under them. I am a Christian, and I know well that the Church and the Cross have often been invoked to justify oppression, genocide, and abuse. I know, also, the long and complex history of the Church, and the times when that institution and its symbols have been used to nonviolently and powerfully resist oppression, to protect the victims of war and persecution, to rescue and to heal. If there is a parallel history of work for racial justice—or indeed any kind of justice for all—under the Confederate flag, I have not seen it yet.

Notes

1   G. Grandin, "The Confederate Flag at War: But Not the Civil War," *Portside*, 7 July 2015, 9.

2   D. Lehr, "The Racist Legacy of Woodrow Wilson," *The Atlantic*, 27 November 2015.

3   P. Leigh, "Okinawa Confederate Flag," *Abbeville Blog*, 6 April 2018, https://www.abbevilleinstitute.org/blog/okinawa-confederate-flag/.

4   G. Grandin, "What Was the Confederate Flag Doing in Cuba, Vietnam and Iraq?," *Nation*, 7 July 2015.

5   M. Martin, "Calley's Civil War," *Abbeville Blog*, 15 March 2018.

6   Grandin, "What Was the Confederate Flag Doing?"

7   Ibid.; see also T. Golden, "In US Report, Brutal Details of 2 Afghan Inmates' Deaths," *New York Times*, 20 May 2005.

8   Statement from the President General, 21 August 2017, United Daughters of the Confederacy, https://hqudc.org/.

9   Lt. General S. D. Lee, "Charge to the Sons of Confederate Veterans, April 25, 1906," *Sons of Confederate Veterans*, scvtexas.org/What_Is_The_SCV.html.

10   Mitch Landrieu, *In the Shadow of Statues: A White Southerner Confronts History* (New York: Viking Press, 2018).

11   Thomas V. Strain Jr., "General Order 2017-01," *Sons of Confederate Veterans*, fraziercamp.org/wp/wp-content/uploads/2017/10/2017-10-Frazier-Camp-Newsletter-October-2017.pdf.

12   Sons of Confederate Veterans, Facebook page, https://www.facebook.com/SCVOfficialPage/.

13   F. Powell, "Confederate Groups Have the Right to Gather in Peace," *News & Observer*, 8 February 2019.

14   Lydia O'Connor and Daniel Marans, "Here Are 13 Examples of Donald Trump Being Racist," *Huffington Post*, 29 February 2016; on Sessions generally, see Matt Bewig, "Attorney General of the United States: Who Is Jeff Sessions," *Allgov*, 29 November 2016, http://www.allgov.com/news/top-stories/attorney-general-of-the-united-states-who-is-jeff-sessions-161129?news=859838.

15   See *The General Condition of the Alabama Negro* (Student Non Violent Coordinating Committee, 1965), ii, https://www.crmvet.org/docs/sncc_al.pdf.

16   *United States v. Wilcox County (Ala.) Board of Education*, 494 F.2d 575 (5th Cir. 1974); *United States v. Wilcox County (Ala.) Board of Education* (DOJ Trial Brief, 1966); see https://www.clearinghouse.net/chDocs/public/SD-AL-0011-0001.pdf.

17   John Sharp, "What They Are Saying about Jeff Sessions Back Home," AL.com, 20 November 2016, https://www.al.com/news/mobile/2016/11/what_they_are_saying_about_jef.html; Maria Gitin, *This Bright Light of Ours: Stories from the Voting Rights Fight* (Tuscaloosa: University of Alabama Press, 2014).

18   Maria Gitin, "Wilcox County AL Churches: Sanctuaries & Action Centers in the Civil Rights Movement," https://www.crmvet.org/comm/gitin14.htm.

19   Fred D. Gray, *Bus Ride to Justice: Changing the System by the System*, rev. ed. (Montgomery, AL: NewSouth Books, 2013), 283.

20   Sarah Wildman, "Jeff Sessions's Chequered Past," *Guardian*, 5 May 2009.

21   "Sessions Subordinate: I Thought I'd Be Fired if I Objected to Being Called 'Boy,'" *Talking Points Memo*, 7 May 2009, https://talkingpointsmemo.com/dc/sessions-subordinate-i-thought-i-d-be-fired-if-i-objected-to-being-called-boy; Jud Lounsbury, "The Sessions Sessions: As Unsettling as You Thought They'd Be," *Progressive*, 11 January 2017, https://progressive.org/dispatches/the-sessions-sessions-as-unsettling-as-you-thought-they-d-be/.

22   Lee Fang, "Senator: Confederate Flag Removal an Attempt to Delegitimize 'Fabulous Accomplishments,'" *Intercept*, 29 June 2015, https://theintercept.com/2015/06/29/push-remove-confederate-flag/ (emphasis added).

23   See Jeff Poor, "Sessions on Confederate Flag Flap: 'It Is Not Appropriate for Us to Erase History,'" *Breitbart*, 29 June 2015, https://www.breitbart.com/clips/2015/06/29/sessions-on-confederate-flag-flap-it-is-not-appropriate-for-us-to-erase-history/.

24 Shannon Sullivan and Nancy Tuana, eds., *Race and Epistemologies of Ignorance* (Albany: SUNY Press, 2007), 1–2.

25 Charles Mills, "White Ignorance," in Sullivan and Tuana, *Race and Epistemologies of Ignorance*, 28–29.

26 Ibid., 30.

27 W.E.B. Du Bois, "The Souls of White Folk" (1920), in *W.E.B. Du Bois: A Reader*, ed. David Levering Lewis (New York: Henry Holt, 1993), 459.

28 S. Francis, "Statement of Principles," *Council of Concerned Citizens*, www.splcenter.org/fighting-hate/extremist-files/group/council-conservative-citizens.

29 Tessa Berenson, "Candidate Trump Said He Would Take Down a Confederate Flag," *Time*, 18 August 2017, https://time.com/4907348/donald-trump-confederate-statues-flags/.

30 Paige Lavender, "Donald Trump 'Sad to See' Confederate Monuments Being Taken Down," *Huffington Post*, 17 August 2017, https://www.huffpost.com/entry/donald-trump-confederate-monuments_n_59959586e4b06ef724d6c37a.

31 "Explaining Why the Confederate Battle Flag Showed Up at Trump Rallies," *Anniston Star*, 22 November 2016, https://www.annistonstar.com/opinion/hotblast/explaining-why-the-confederate-battle-flag-showed-up-at-trump/article_c484ec20-b02f-11e6-b210-039e64a69035.html.

32 D. Boroff, "'It's Racism': Counter-Protestors Stand against Confederate Flag Displays about Michigan High School," *New York Daily News*, 18 April 2018.

33 E. Doran, "CNY School Bans Confederate Flag, Suspends Students for Displaying It," *Syracuse.com*, 7 April 2017.

34 L. Acker, "Confederate Flag Hangs in Men's Co-Op across from Black Cultural Center in Corvallis," *Oregonian*, 20 September 2017.

35 J.D. Armour, "The Politics of Becoming," *BLARB*, 19 January 2016.

36 Ibid.

37 Zinn, *People's History*, 207.

38 Egerton, *The Wars of Reconstruction*, 168.

39 Isabel Wilkerson, *The Warmth of Other Suns* (New York: Vintage, 2010).

40 "Buffalo Ku Klux Klan Membership List," New York Heritage Digital Collections, www.nyheritage.org/collections/buffalo-ku-klux-klan-membership-list.

41 B. Axelson, "KKK Flyers with Valentine's Day Theme Shock Residents in Upstate NY City," *NYUp*, 12 February 2018; "Ku Klux Klan Flyers Spur New York Investigation," *Governing.com*, 7 August 2018.

42 D. Morgan, "Ga. Confederate Flag Supporters Face Terrorism Charges," *CBS News*, 12 October 2015.

43   Mayra Cuevas and Ralph Ellis, "Georgia Couple Gets Prison for Racist Threats at Child's Birthday Party," CNN, 1 March 2017.

44   H. Peterson and C. Campbell, "Confederate Flag Sales Are Skyrocketing," *Business Insider*, 23 June 2015; R. Layne, "Confederate Flag Sales Are Booming after Charlottesville," *CBS News*, 25 August 2017.

45   C.K. Chumley, "Charlottesville Fallout: Confederate Flag Sales Hike," *Washington Times*, 24 August 2017.

Chapter Eight

THE RATIONALE FOR COLIN KAEPERNICK'S MORAL STANCE

IT'S A FAMILIAR IMAGE BY NOW: COLIN KAEPERNICK kneeling on the gridiron, garbed in scarlet and gold. Around him, a solemn crowd stands with their hands pressed to their chests, affirming their love of country for all to see. Hoisted high above their heads is an American flag, majestic and pristine, fluttering in the breeze. For many Americans, these images have an intoxicating effect. Their juxtaposition taps into something visceral. There is no more quintessentially American pastime than football, no emblem more American than Old Glory, and no act more American than rising to one's feet for a rendition of the Star-Spangled Banner. It is the deep entrenchment of these symbols that makes the idea of an American football hero refusing to honor the flag of his country particularly jarring.

Which was, presumably, the point.

The ritual surrounding the performance of the national anthem at American sporting events is more than just symbolic patriotism:

it is participatory patriotism. From a young age, we Americans have been expected to take part in this uniform display of unconditional solidarity. We may participate with apathy, slumping and staring off into the distance, or we may participate with ardor, standing ramrod-straight, chin jutting forward, gazing upon the stars and stripes, but the one inviolable rule is that we must participate.

Since our national anthem is a hymn to the purity of American harmony and *esprit de corps*, or so the thinking goes, its rendition is an opportunity for reflection upon the sacrifices of those who came before us. Such a moment is no time to call attention to something as divisive and contentious as the unequal application of justice in America.

Yes, of course, equality matters. But a football game is no place for such antics. In reality, it is the perfect place, and Kaepernick's choice of venue for his nonviolent protest was as shrewd as it was obvious, given his profession. With the eyes of his nation fixed upon him, there could have been no better time or place to call attention to one of that nation's most egregious failings.

Many were less than appreciative of this reminder, of course. Of all the people who waxed indignant about Kaepernick's decision to kneel during the national anthem, it was the fiery reaction of self-avowed patriots that was the most incoherent, and the most telling ... if also the most predictable. These people derided Kaepernick as ungrateful, as un-American, and as a coward. They ignored—or perhaps genuinely failed to comprehend—the remarkable courage it required for Kaepernick to consciously step into the path of the rushing freight train that is American patriotic sanctimony: to stand on those tracks, alone at first, knowing that the force barreling down on him was unstoppable and unforgiving.

In another context, many of Kaepernick's detractors would see such unflinching self-sacrifice, undertaken at great personal and professional risk and solely for the good of his countrymen, as the very definition of heroism. In this context, however—an uninvited encroachment on a hallowed ritual, and on their weekly Budweiser bacchanalia—Kaepernick's act of protest was viewed not as heroism but as insolence. His detractors also ignored the fact that the price of Kaepernick's gesture was relatively modest from the perspective of historic civil resistance. It is difficult to imagine a single act of political dissent that could have had such widespread visibility, which could have been so widely imitated,[1] and which could have stoked such vigorous debate without shedding a single drop of blood. It is equally difficult to imagine a response to systemic injustice that is more wholly American. It was an unmistakable act of patriotism—and one that few public figures have recognized as such.[2]

To the sort of people who called for Kaepernick's head, however, patriotism is a simple, rigid concept. It is not some high-minded philosophy to be refined and wrestled with: it is a glittering cloak to be draped over the shoulders of cherished heroes. Patriotism is a thing to be flaunted and flourished, like a matador waving his cape. To toss that cape aside, for any reason whatsoever, is to deserve the goring that will inevitably follow, and worse. Such an act is not a mere political statement: it is a repudiation of America itself, and is tantamount to treason.

But real patriotism is more than a prop to be dragged out of the closet on game day, and more than a pin to be fastened to a lapel. It is more than the stars and stripes, or the drum and the fife. It runs deeper than the mere symbols that represent it. Symbolism is not an inherently negative thing. In fact, it can work both ways.[3] In America, a nation built on powerful symbolism, there is no more potent catalyst for change than a bold symbolic act. Throughout American history—from the signing of the Declaration of Independence to the solitary civil disobedience of Rosa Parks—symbolic acts have inspired meaningful change.

Symbolic patriotism can also have a healing effect, as it did in the aftermath of 9/11. But sometimes symbolism is camouflage, and sometimes symbolic patriotism is camouflage of a particularly dishonest and harmful sort. One of the core problems with the more simplistic, dogmatic form of patriotism embraced by Kaepernick's detractors is that at its base lies an innate loathing of otherness. The objects of such loathing, and the recipients of its rotting fruits, are, as ever, those who are different.

More simply put, this shallower form of patriotism often draws from the same deep well as racial hatred and discrimination, and it yields similar results. This jingoistic streak is a very human trait. It has served humankind well and was perhaps a critical contributor to the evolution and survival of the human species in prehistoric times, when any out-group could represent an existential threat.[4] In a modern, multi-ethnic society, however, it is a barrier to progress. Humanity is no longer confined to small tribes fighting for survival on a sub-Saharan veld or in walled city-states in the Fertile Crescent. We are billions strong, inextricably interconnected, and our numbers increase each year. The option of isolating ourselves from others no longer exists. We Americans must live together, and in order to do so in peace and prosperity we must all have equal footing under the law. This necessity is as non-negotiable as it is uroboric; the survival of our democracy hinges on equality, and the fight for equality hinges upon the uniform, impartial application of democracy.

But that is not happening in Colin Kaepernick's America. Instead of equal protection under the law, a large subset of America's citizenry requires equal protection *from* the law, or at least from those who enforce the law. Being a police officer in America is dangerous, but being black in America is more dangerous still.[5] This dichotomy—that some Americans are protected by law enforcement while others are brutalized by it—is increasingly untenable, and its very existence flies in the face of the notion of American freedom. This truth should be self-evident, but it seems lost on many in the flag-waving set. These people, who consider the various freedoms articulated in the Constitution to be inalienable rights, fail to comprehend that the instant those rights are legally denied to *any* American, of *any* background or ethnicity, they are no longer inalienable.[6] If the government protects the rights of only some Americans, then the government effectively becomes the proprietor of those rights. These rights, which America's Founders considered to be endowed by their Creator, instead become forbearances granted by the state: arbitrary favors bestowed on some but withheld from others. Anything so granted by an authority that has a monopoly on force can be taken away by that same authority: not just from some Americans, but from all of us. If any American is stripped of their civil rights, then every American's rights are under assault.

And yet the civil rights of certain Americans *are* violated, repeatedly and often unapologetically, with disturbing regularity. The violations are severely lopsided in terms of the racial makeup of their victims, disproportionately victimizing Americans of color.[7] But the race or ethnicity of the victims is not the point. The fact that *any* American's civil rights are being eroded or ignored means that the intrinsic value of those rights, for every person who lays claim to them, is diminished. With this in mind, all American patriots, of any size, shape, color, or background, should be seething in fury with every new transgression by law enforcement against *any* American citizen, not only on behalf of the victim but also on behalf of the soul of the nation they claim to love. Any reaction short of outrage does damage and dishonor to America's core precepts.

And yet this all-too-common occurrence meets with apathy or acceptance by Americans who otherwise consider themselves patriots. That such people prefer to reserve their outrage for something as relatively innocuous as an act of silent protest during a football game only compounds the insult. An American football player with one knee planted on the AstroTurf should not rouse more fury than an unarmed, bullet-riddled American teenager gasping out his last breath on the asphalt of a St. Louis suburb.

And yet it does. Why?

Part of the answer—the part that doesn't include racism or the alarming militarization of America's police[8]—is a desire for simplicity. The latter instance requires deeper contemplation. Too many connections must be made in order to fully comprehend that this teenager's death is a stark violation of the American ideal. Humans in general tend to simplify complicated matters, and Americans in particular seem increasingly averse to nuance in their public discourse. It is much simpler to react to a symbolic affront than to a deeper, more complex one.

But this explanation only goes so far. The reaction among this same segment of society to the Black Lives Matter movement helps to further fill in the blanks. Instead of an acknowledgment of the concern that the lives of black Americans were being treated by the justice system as something of lesser value, these folks offered the snide riposte that *All Lives Matter*, either misunderstanding or, more likely, willfully ignoring that the phrase *black lives matter* was simply an abbreviated exhortation of the obvious fact that *black lives matter too.*[9]

The underpinning of Black Lives Matter was the simple, intuitive contention that a black life should be valued on par with every other American life, and that when such a life is snuffed out without due cause, the indignation among all Americans should run as high as if the victim's eyes were blue and his skin were white. Racial apathy aside, this reaction—or lack of one—suggests that one of the greatest perils of symbolic, flag-waving patriotism is that it can displace the deeper, more consequential class of philosophical patriotism upon which this nation's founding principles were based. American-flag bumper stickers and chanted affirmations of allegiance are poor substitutes for learning, vigilance, and civic action.

At its best, patriotism can be an elevated thing, a national philosophy based on careful examination of oneself, of one's compatriots, and of history. This sort of reasoned altruism is the bedrock of the American experiment. At its worst, however, patriotism is impulsive and superficial, a throwback to our most primitive instincts. This latter sort of patriotism—actually pseudo-patriotism—is simply lazy, since a deeper understanding of America's founding values can be obtained from any high-school history textbook. President Trump's vitriolic condemnation of Kaepernick exemplifies this variety of pseudo-patriotism and provides a textbook example of bad-faith politics. Despite what this simplistic view suggests, American patriotism should never be confined to a reverence for a colorful piece of cloth, or for a stirring piece of music. Nor should it be confined to a regard for the men and women who have fought in our wars.

Patriotism is about love of the country itself, not exaltation of the military that defends it. Moreover, it is not just this nation's fighters who have made sacrifices for its future. Many of the Founders whom today we revere as heroes never faced a musket or a cannon. Some were indeed fighters, like George Washington, but many were writers and thinkers, like Benjamin Franklin, Thomas Jefferson, and John Adams. A few, like Alexander Hamilton, were both. Yet, fighter or thinker, statesman or orator, these men have spent the last two centuries lauded as heroes because they were willing to stand up to a status quo that treated them as second-class citizens, and to a government who refused to afford them the same rights and representation as their countrymen.

The parallel to Kaepernick, when viewed in this light, is quite nearly perfect. It's true that the Founders signed their name to a document that might, if their rebellion failed, be waved in front of their own noses as they stood at the gallows. But what most of them actually sacrificed was not their blood but their livelihood. Washington, Hamilton, and Adams in particular would have been wealthier by far if they had chosen a less obstreperous path.[10] Yet they didn't, and the legacy of their courage, and that of all of the American Founders, is with us still.

So, too, is their other legacy: a deep national disposition toward cognitive dissonance with regard to race. Some of the Founders, even as they extolled the virtues and imperatives of personal freedom, depended for their own subsistence on the toil, misery, and involuntary servitude of others. These others, no less American, were not free, and never would be. Their mothers and fathers had been enslaved, as would be their sons and daughters. The profound, historic, and hitherto novel assertion that all men were created equal did not, in the minds of the Americans who first articulated it, mean that all men should be treated accordingly. Some, by virtue of their otherness, could be subjugated, enslaved, and brutalized with impunity.

Two centuries later, after a grueling, often bloody national journey that has so frequently seemed destined to rip this country apart, this baffling legacy of cognitive dissonance is still very much in evidence. Somehow, in spite of all the advancements of Western society and in spite of all the blood that has been spilled, a certain segment of our society is still allowed to be brutalized with relative impunity, and a certain other segment of our society still views this as permissible. It would be specious to claim that the level of today's brutality is on par with that meted out to people of color during America's founding years, but that distinction is scant comfort to those being brutalized, or to the families of unarmed victims slain by the armed proxies of a government tasked with their protection and well-being.

For Kaepernick to stand up for these victims—or, more accurately, to kneel for them amid the hue and cry of an enraged multitude, and at the expense of his own livelihood—is a classic example of American courage. It may not be on par with some of history's more noteworthy acts of civil disobedience in terms of personal peril, but the idea that it is somehow cowardly or self-serving makes little sense unless you are viewing things on the most surface level.

That is, perhaps, the core of the problem. Americans have been force-fed patriotism for so long that we have come to view it as something to be consumed rather than something to be deliberated and enlarged upon, or as something to be perfunctorily celebrated rather than vigorously exercised. For any meaningful progress to occur in the American political discourse, this must change. While it may be futile to expect rank-and-file Americans to spend their evenings poring over the *Federalist Papers* or pondering Locke's *Two Treatises*, the case for a deeper class of American patriotism is not hopeless. It requires a more careful blending of symbolic patriotism with a deeper appreciation for what lies beneath.

Symbols do matter, for the simple fact that humans respond to them. Symbols are how we communicate.[11] The words you are reading right now are merely a complex arrangement of symbols. To categorize the human impulse to grasp at symbols as primitive or too simplistic, therefore, is to miss the point, and to squander an opportunity. The Founders knew the power of symbols, but they also knew that, for such power to be relevant, a symbol must be understood to represent something deeper. For many Americans, this distinction seems to have been lost. They have allowed the trappings of patriotism to supplant patriotism itself. To have any hope of broadening this narrow view of patriotism, we must first understand its origins. To posit that superficial patriotism arises solely from ignorance or apathy—while it might very well involve both—is neither helpful nor sufficiently precise.

As mentioned above, there are evincible reasons for humans to have evolved the capacity for such parochialism: the early survival of our species probably hinged, in part, on a narrow definition of which people warranted trust and which did not. Any expansion of that definition would have been a dangerous proposition.

This capacity still exists in all of us, but it seems particularly evident in those who exhibit an ideological variable called *right-wing authoritarianism*. It is worth noting that this term itself is apolitical and that authoritarians exist all along the political continuum, including the political left, although in modern America they are most strongly represented on the political right.[12]

As early human societies swelled in size from small tribes and clans to vast, sprawling nations, the ability to limit the size of our in-groups diminished. The emotional need for the security of an insular group still exists, however, and the right-wing authoritarian (RWA) satisfies this need through an affinity for uniformity. In the absence of a small, tight-knit group, uniformity can help make a dangerous, uncertain existence feel safer and more predictable and can help to simplify a world that often seems staggeringly complex.

The problem with these attempts to simplify the world around us is that they are rooted in fantasy.[13] The world *is* a complex place, whether we accept that fact or not. In order for the intellect to accommodate such an abridgment of reality, important concessions must be made, and critical nuances must be ignored. In particular, integrative complexity—the ability to see the same matter from multiple perspectives—must be viewed not as a strength but as a weakness, born not of intellectual rigor but of a wishy-washy lack of resolve.[14] This naturally creates an us-versus-them mentality, where divergence is perceived as arising not from a difference of opinion but from a place of malignance or stupidity.

It's not just political ideology that is in play here, however. Anyone who breaks the pattern of uniformity, whether of ideology, language, or physical appearance, is a potential enemy with the potential to undermine social order. In the mind of the RWA, in order to combat these enemies and protect societal uniformity, it is often necessary to anoint a savior.[15] At the national level, this usually means electing a president who espouses law and order—without regard for whether that president actually observes or exemplifies these things in his own life—and whose stated philosophy reflects the RWA's own blinkered outlook.

On this national level, their deep-seated need for security exposes the RWA to easy manipulation, a phenomenon I discuss briefly below. Because they identify with a leader who exhibits strength, the RWAs are able to see themselves as strong too. Lost on them, apparently, is the fact that they are submitting to a relationship of subservience—and often self-abasement—with a strong father figure. Instead of confronting difficulties themselves, they hand the job over to a strongman. In this way, they epitomize not strength but weakness, not patriotism but a betrayal of the freedom and self-reliance that is most quintessentially American.

This is difficult for them to see, however. Likewise, since their professions of love for America are based on superficial demonstrations of patriotism, they assume that any who refuse to engage in such demonstrations must not love America. This outlook is facile, to be sure, but for someone who is unwilling or unable to contemplate patriotism as a layered philosophy, this cause-and-effect relationship is inescapable. No deeper reasoning can justify an outward show of disrespect, not because it threatens America but because it diminishes the uniformity and security they value above all else.

While Kaepernick's protest sparked patriotic fury on the national level, its roots were at the local level. If the RWA's savior figure on the national level is a law-and-order president, on the local level it is a tough, no-nonsense cop. The upper branches of government create our laws, but it is the local cop who enforces them and maintains order. Likewise, it is here, on the cop's beat, that the pseudo-patriotic RWA's existential anxiety is most readily transformed into injustice, because it is here that the source of his primeval fear—the "other" who exists outside his narrow definition of trust—actually lives.

Just as they will circle their wagons to defend the indefensible on the national stage, they will rally to the defense of their local saviors too, often regardless of the accusations leveled against them. Even if video footage exists that clearly shows a police officer emptying his weapon into a fleeing, unarmed civilian, as in the 2015 case of Walter Scott,[16] there will be a contingent willing to explain away the officer's actions. This will be a comparatively modest percentage, perhaps, but a troubling number nonetheless—especially since most would consider themselves patriots, and most would agree that one of America's core precepts is freedom from tyranny.

To the person who reflexively defends the police, the problem of police misconduct is simply nonexistent. Those who are most vocal about the evils of police malfeasance, they assure themselves, are ideologues bent on excusing flaws, faults, and shortcomings within their own communities. If "those people" would only [*insert corrective measure here*], then the police would have no need to brutalize them. This is patently false, of course. While there is certainly such a thing as agitation for political or personal gain, there is also a point at which it should become obvious to any reasonable onlooker that a real problem exists.

In the same tract that contains Samuel Johnson's shopworn quotation that calls patriotism the "refuge of scoundrels," he articulates the difference between these two perspectives: "The true lover of his country is ready to communicate his fears, and to sound the alarm, whenever he perceives the approach of mischief. But he sounds no alarm when there is no enemy; he never terrifies his countrymen till he is terrified himself."[17]

That this disparity of perspective exists speaks to the underlying problem that Kaepernick's protests helped to lay bare. To be white in America is to have the luxury of assuming that most such alarms are false, since there are so many of them, and since so few lead to convictions of the purported perpetrator, and since most white Americans have not experienced any of this supposed injustice themselves.

To be black in America, on the other hand, is to be afforded no such luxury. To be black in America—especially to be young, male, and black, or the parent of such—is to wrestle with a constant undercurrent of dread that one's life and future are subject to the whim of a person in a position of authority who may not see you as a member of their in-group, and who may be operating under the assumption that you are his enemy. While this in no way describes all police officers, a growing number of whom are people of color themselves, it is based on a very real perception that is easily confirmed by statistical evidence.[18]

To be black in America today is, as per Johnson, to be terrified—or at least to exist in a situation where being terrified is a perfectly rational response. Before the advent of smartphones, a lack of credulity regarding this matter was perhaps more defensible. Today, however, every American has access to a constant stream of compelling evidence supporting longstanding claims by the black community of police misconduct.

This is a positive shift in the dynamic, to be sure. For the average person, a video of a citizen of any ethnicity being murdered in cold blood by a police officer is indeed enough on its own to incite indignation and horror. For the RWA, however—particularly one who has no firsthand experience with injustice—there is usually an assumption of some extenuating context that absolves the perpetrator of his actions and shifts the blame to the victim. Whether that extenuating context actually exists seems to be less important to the RWA than buttressing their own pre-existing worldview.

With regard to some recent cases of police abuse—like that of Walter Scott—the intellectual contortion necessary to excuse the perpetrator borders on miraculous. Even with incidents for which no video evidence exists, however—assuming the most charitable scenario, where the RWA has a basic level of human decency—the unconscionability of lethal violence perpetrated upon any unarmed citizen should be self-evident.

To countenance such an act, therefore, it is necessary to alter the narrative surrounding it, usually by foisting the responsibility for acts of violence upon the victims themselves. To justify the murder of Trayvon Martin, for instance, he must not be seen as a conventional teenager who smoked a little weed and dreamed of a career in aviation; he must be relegated to a frightening stereotype, and recreated as a menacing, hoodie-wearing thug with a history of violence and a troubling criminal background.[19] Such a person is, according to the RWA mindset, deserving of punishment merely by virtue of his own nature.

While this propensity to strip others of their personhood is a very human trait, it has manifested itself throughout history in appallingly inhuman ways. Likewise, the desire—or perhaps the need—for uniformity that is the defining characteristic of the pseudo-patriot is also the defining characteristic of human history's most murderous political movements.[20] Anyone who thinks of themselves as a patriot would chafe at this comparison, but the susceptibility of the RWA to manipulation was brought front-and-center in the presidential election of 2016, when a notorious swindler was able to convince a large swath of the American electorate that, in spite of much contradictory evidence, he was a person who loved America, and that he was the only person who could save a nation that was being undermined from within and overrun from without. He was even able to convince committed Christians that he was himself a religious man, despite clear and overwhelming evidence to the contrary.

The appalling absurdity of his candidacy notwithstanding, the ruse worked. Once he secured the nomination, he was embraced by shrewd politicians, themselves skilled manipulators of patriotic fervor (although some ethical members of his party were willing to oppose his rise). This incapable, conspicuously amoral pretender was elevated to the highest office in the land largely by appealing to people who see America as having a fixed identity that is conveniently one which most closely resembles their own family and social circle, and who are willing to ignore the historical consequences of electing such a leader.

In short, he wielded their own patriotism—and their own insecurities—against them.

Support for such a person reeks of ignorance and desperation, and it might be considered comical or cartoonish until we remember that some of history's most murderous leaders have been viewed as such by those outside their target demographic—but only initially, before they solidified real power. In any case, it is not the person who perceives the obvious absurdity of this situation that the demagogue is attempting to manipulate. Instead, his target is the mind of the pseudo-patriot, often untempered by the critical thinking that is instilled through higher education—which is not, by any means, the same thing as stupidity, but rather an inability to remove their own bias from their thought process[21]—and his goal is to draw them into the sort of feedback loop that has spun the intellectual fog America now finds itself in, which entails the embrace of a simplistic, hidebound version of pseudo-patriotism that is isolated from any wider context, and whose adherents are therefore ripe for further manipulation. Once trust is established, all the demagogue has to do is push the same button, over and over again, to get what he wants.

Kaepernick's protest provided America's demagogues with one such button. While it did serve its intended purpose as a jarring reminder for many Americans, it also provided a useful tool through which to manipulate a significant number of them.

If the American experiment is to continue in any meaningful sense, we must work to reverse this congenital vulnerability in the American psyche, and in order to do that we must accept that Kaepernick's symbolic act—like all acts of protest—was merely a take-off point.

Like other symbolic acts of civil disobedience, the movement Kaepernick spawned will have little effect on its own beyond the conversation and debate it has already stirred. Already, in the years since he first took a knee, the furor engendered by his defiance has begun to fade. The image of an American athlete kneeling to the opening strains of the national anthem, so potent only a few years ago, has lost its bite. Kaepernick's resistance has been imitated by others, initially amplifying its power but inevitably diffusing it as well. Megan Rapinoe, the American soccer player who in 2016 began kneeling as a show of solidarity with Kaepernick[22]—and who, now that kneeling has been prohibited, still refuses to place her hand over her heart during renditions of the anthem—often directs the consequent attention to other areas of deep injustice, from LGBTQ rights to gender discrimination in her own sport.

This sort of dispersal is the ineluctable fate of all token acts. That's not necessarily a bad thing, for surely Kaepernick's isolated defiance was never intended to comprise the totality of a movement. It was not in itself an act of war but rather a solitary rocket fired across the bow of America's conflicted conscience: a distress flare meant to assure some of us—and to remind the rest of us—that our cherished flag means nothing without the ideals for which it stands, and that the indomitable resolve of the men who first hoisted that flag toward the heavens is as needful today as it ever was.

In other words, for Kaepernick's protest to have any lasting effect, further action is required. The protest itself is not enough to fix our problems. It was not the Declaration of Independence that freed our Founders from the yoke of British tyranny—the Revolution did that. It was not Rosa Parks's act of courage in Montgomery, Alabama, that codified racial equality—the *Civil Rights Act* did that. Each of the former helped catalyze the later outcome, but neither was enough on its own.

Likewise, without applying pressure to the levers of real power—from the local police departments to the national legislature and judiciary—and without a national conversation about what patriotism actually means—the image of a kneeling football player may end up being nothing more than a passing historical curiosity. Kaepernick has hurled his hail-Mary pass downfield, but it will be up to others to snatch it from the air and transport it, by whatever means they can, into the end zone.

* * *

If, as Socrates opined, the unexamined life is not worth living, surely unexamined national ardor is not worth having. Love of country, like the love of anything worth caring for, must be based on more than empty attestations. It must acknowledge that country's flaws, or it is of little value. If patriotism is rigid, it will atrophy. It must be flexed, passionately and frequently, and it must be challenged and re-evaluated at every turn.

To achieve the elevated class of patriotism mentioned above will require a willingness to engage in real introspection: a willingness not only on the part of those who clamor for change but also on the part of those who fear change. For this to begin to happen, the latter group must be shaken out of its pseudo-patriotic stupor. It may be uncomfortable, and it will make some of them angry, but it is necessary.

In this respect, Kaepernick's act of defiance was a service rendered to all Americans, though some did not ask for it and might never be capable of recognizing its value. His service was to show that the pure, unblemished flag that so gallantly streams above our most hallowed national events represents a land that is neither pure nor unblemished, and whose citizens are neither uniformly brave nor wholly free.

Until America's deepest flaws are addressed, our nation would more accurately be represented by a flag whose colors are fading, and whose fabric, tattered and threadbare, is in desperate need of mending.

Notes

1   A. Harris, "The Fight of Their Lives," *B/R Mag*, 26 September 2016.

2   J. Hill, "Beto O'Rourke Grabbed a Political Third Rail—and Electrified His Campaign," *The Atlantic*, 27 October 2018.

3   T.D. Oyedemi, "Protest as Communication for Demonstration of Social Change," https://link.springer.com/content/pdf/10.1007/978-981-10-7035-8_132-1.pdf.

4   E. Culotta, "Roots of Rascism," *Science*, 18 May 2012.

5   R. Brooks, "America's Police Problem Isn't Just about Police," *FP*, 5 January 2016.

6   Judith Blau and Alberto Moncada, *Justice in the United States* (Plymouth, UK: Rowman and Littlefield, 2006).

7   Amnesty International, *Deadly Force* (New York: Amnesty International USA, 2015).

8   J. Munnola, "Militarization Fails to Enhance Police Safety or Reduce Crime but May Harm Police Reputation," *PNAS*, 11 September 2018.

9   Ashley Atkins, "*Black Lives Matter* or *All Lives Matter*? Color-blindness and Epistemic Injustice," *Social Epistemology* 33.1 (2019): 1–22.

10   W.S. Randall, "Washington Was Broke? Why Founding Fathers Were Strapped for Cash," *Daily Beast*, 13 July 2017.

11   C.D. Vallotten and C. Ayoub, "Symbols Build Communication and Thought: The Role of Gestures and Words in the Development of Engagement Skills and Social-Emotional Concepts during Toddlerhood," *Social Development* 19.2 (2011): 601–26.

12   Bob Altemeyer, *The Authoritarians* (2006), audio book available at www.audible.co.uk.

13   R.C. Giambatista, J.D. Hoover, and L. Tribble, "Millennials, Learning, and Development: Managing Complexity Avoidance and Narcissism," *Psychologist-Manager Journal* 20.3 (2017): 176–93.

14   P.E. Tetlock, "Cognitive Style and Political Ideology," *Journal of Personality and Social Psychology* 45.1 (1983): 118–26.

15   N. LeTourneau, "Christian Nationalists Have Made Trump Their Savior," *Washington Monthly*, 22 March 2019.

16   A. Blinder, "Michael Slager, Officer in Walter Scott Shooting, Gets 20-Year Sentence," *New York Times*, 7 December 2017.

17   Samuel Johnson, "The Patriot" (1774), in *The Works of Samuel Johnson* (Troy, NY: Pafraets & Company, 1913), vol. 14, 81–93.

18   G. Lopez, "There Are Huge Racial Disparities in How US Police Use Force," *Vox*, 14 November 2018.

19   Y. Alcindor, "Trayvon Martin: Typical Teen or Troublemaker?," *USA Today*, 11 December 2012.

20   Carlos de la Torre, "Trump's Populism: Lessons from Latin America," *Postcolonial Studies* 20.2 (2017): 1–12.

21   M. Motta, "The Dynamics and Political Implications of Anti-Intellectualism in the United States," *American Politics Research* 46.3 (2017): 465–98.

22   M. Rapinoe, "Why I Am Kneeling," *Players Tribune*, 6 October 2016.

AFTERWORD

THROUGHOUT WESTERN HISTORY, WE HAVE WALKED through the valley of the shadow of death only to learn that some shadows are yet darker, yet more terrifying and gruesome than death: the shadows of poxes and plagues, of slavery and subjugation, of holy war and holocaust. Now, as before, we find ourselves confronting one such shadow—the fathomless shadow of self-annihilation. Staring into this abyss is dizzying and terrifying, because, to paraphrase Friedrich Nietzsche, it stares with increasing intensity back at us, beckoning us, daring us to take that final leap into a nothingness that precludes both resurrection and salvation.

We have arrived here, have looked down to see ourselves inches from the edge of annihilation, because we believe in this country, but we hold very different ideas about what and for whom she was founded. We call this the Land of the Free, but whose freedom? If we say "Freedom for all," we show a poor understanding of our history.

The Land of the Free was never intended for everyone. From its inception, the United States has practiced bad faith in terms of guaranteeing freedom for all who call this land home. After all, this country was built on the backs of African slaves, atop the bones of Native Americans. The former saw themselves stolen from their homes; the latter witnessed their ancestral lands and hunting grounds appropriated through force and subterfuge. A policy of aggression defined our country's rapid expansion, peaking with the Mexican-American War. In 1846, after his efforts to purchase Mexican territory were rebuffed, President Polk decided to use force. Polk ordered American troops to march into a disputed zone within the Mexican state of Coahuila, and Mexico responded to this invasion as any country would: it engaged the American forces with forces of their own.

After this skirmish and a couple of subsequent battles, Polk went before Congress to make the case for war. He said, "The cup of forbearance has been exhausted, even before Mexico passed the boundary of the United States, invaded our territory, and shed American blood upon American soil." Congress promptly declared war, and American troops invaded a sovereign nation in order to steal its land. Bolstered with superior rifles and other technology, the Americans soundly beat the Mexicans at every turn, laid siege to Mexico City, and forced the signing of a treaty that landed them half of Mexico's territory.

In this instance, a young but powerful nation invaded a weaker one and asserted its will. Polk's speech to Congress was riddled with lies and misrepresentations. As for the general public, it zealously backed the president. How could a people that purport to cherish freedom and self-determination support brazen aggression against a sovereign neighbor? The justification for this hypocrisy is simple: racism. Polk emphasized in his speech that "American blood" had been shed. That Mexican blood had also flowed made no difference. American blood had been shed, and that demanded a violent response.

The American public consistently supported expansionist policy, despite the fact that every acre of newly acquired territory was already occupied. Racist ideologies propped up our aggressive expansion. These "inferior races" (Mexican or Native) were considered lazy and cowardly by nature. The United States, as the self-appointed poster-child of intrepid industrialism, could point to its own success as evidence that Native Americans and Mexicans were unfit stewards of their own territory. Annexation was thus excused—indeed, demanded—by our manifest destiny. Ours was a superior culture, a superior people, taking under God's eye that which was destined for us to exploit. This type of racist ideology would later appear with regard to citizens of the Philippines, Guam, Panama, and Hawaii. In other words, if white people wanted some land that belonged to brown people, they had not just the right but the duty to take it.

This was how it was presented to the American people, but surely, many of those who spoke about manifest destiny and about the innate inferiority of those we have subjugated knew that these are hollow ideologies—utterly baseless and utterly meritless. American politicians have long used racism to bait the public into support for policies that would otherwise be defenseless. Did Polk really think that he was simply doing his duty as a white man when he took half of Mexico? Of course not. He wanted to expand America's southern borders. Surely, he didn't do it in defense of her nascent values. He did it for American glory and American profit—not for American values. A nation that crows about liberty for all cannot, without sounding hypocritical, impose its will on its neighbors. This is simply might making right, the age-old phenomenon of the powerful dominating the weak, and, when necessary, justifying subjugation by playing on racist prejudice.

When people celebrate the United States and glorify those who waved her banner in conflicts at home or abroad, they tend to celebrate not a real country and not even real people, but idealized ones. Of course, America (and by extension, the American hero) has different meanings depending on who is speaking. A conservative voter might feel connected to an America of small towns, of staid nuclear families, of "good" wars, and of helpful, likeminded neighbors. A liberal voter, on the other hand, might feel connected to America's founding messages of equality, to her history of multiculturalism, to the great melting pot of cultures and ideas, to this country's much-vaunted push to realize a more perfect union. The first- or second-generation immigrant might be drawn to America's continued position as the "land of opportunity," where hard work and success are synonymous. The white nationalist sees America through a different lens. He sees culture as a product of race, seeing the immigrant as a diluter of this culture, as a parasite actively working to destroy what he sees as the nation's collective interests.

Problems arise due to the oppositional interests of these broadly sketched ideals: those of the conservative vs. the liberal, the immigrant vs. the nationalist. What makes race so problematic is that it sits at the center of both these conflicts. Further problems arise when groups apply their values selectively. The anti-abortion voter, so protective of prenatal life, sees no reason for programs that support postnatal life. The east-coast liberal, pushing always for more seats at a non-discriminatory roundtable, pulls the seat out from under the heartland conservative. The president, spewing rhetoric to court the middle class, signs actual policy to benefit the one per cent. Each of these attitudes constitutes bad faith.

These two concepts—racism and bad faith—intertwine like mating vipers to create progeny that threaten not only our ideals but also the very fabric of our nation. To even dream of a united, multi-racial America, of bright colors and tight seams, we need first to return to some semblance of political sanity. And to do that, we must first find a way to remember how to speak to each other as full Americans, as human beings. This is the antithesis of populism, this is the bane of the populist's dominion.

A multi-racial and ideologically pluralistic democracy, in its best form, needs vision, it demands hope and, like a plant, cannot thrive in darkness. My mentor Cornel West often told me that democracy cannot thrive in nihilism, and I do my best to pass this on in my teaching, preaching, and political witnessing. One path in this nadir called Trumpism is a devolving into darkness, a sort of Good Friday[1] funk that continues into Holy Saturday.[2] It may feel as if we have been through much of this before, but the United States has never looked into an abyss quite like this one. Our history is riddled with events that seem to echo in today's events, but it is important to recognize that we have, in a critical sense, wandered onto untrodden ground.

If we want to truly set things back to rights, it will take something dramatic, but it must also be democratic. It is, so to speak, up to us—we will not be saved by a white-horsed savior. We must do it together. We must cast aside our messianic hopes in favor of a simpler and more flexible hope. We must also, of course, do more than hope, but hope is what allows us to polish our tarnished ideals and rebuild our cherished institutions. Hope tells us that resurrecting our democracy is not only possible but also worthwhile. Cynicism and bad-faith actors are pulling us further and further away from the perfect idea of America (which is, it must be said, not a perfect America, only a perfect idea of a *more* perfect union). Those who will pull us back to the center will be those of conscience, sincerity, and moral courage. We must listen carefully and heed their calls when they come.

We must tune our ears so we can hear not just the good but the bad as well. We must learn to recognize bad faith when we see it, and we must, wherever possible, tear down those edifices of hypocrisy and bad faith and replace them with edifices of truth, straight dealing, and good faith. We face tremendous challenges as a people of faith and conscience. We have faced down similar challenges before, have stared into the abyss without flinching. We must do so again, and to do so, we must renew our faith: our faith in possibility; our faith in democracy; our faith in progress; our faith in each other; our faith in America.

Notes

1   Referring to the historic day on which believers say Christ was crucified.
2   Considered the darkest day in the Christian calendar.

WORKS CITED

Note: This list contains only print and journal sources.

Allen, Theodore W. *The Invention of the White Race*. 2 vols. New York: Verso, 1997.

Altemeyer, Bob. *The Authoritarians* (2006). Audio book available at www.audible. co.uk.

Atkins, Ashley. "*Black Lives Matter* or *All Lives Matter*? Color-blindness and Epistemic Injustice." *Social Epistemology* 33.1 (2019): 1–22.

Bailey, Julius. *Racial Realities and Post-Racial Dreams*. Peterborough, ON: Broadview, 2016.

Barber, Rev. William J., II. *The Third Reconstruction: Moral Monday, Fusion Politics, and the Rise of a New Justice Movement*. Boston: Beacon Press, 2016.

Blau, Judith, and Alberto Moncada. *Justice in the United States*. Plymouth, UK: Rowman and Littlefield, 2006.

Bremmer, Ian. *Us vs. Them: The Failure of Globalism*. New York: Portfolio/Penguin, 2018.

Bullard, Robert D. "Dismantling Environmental Racism in the USA." *Local Environment* 4.1 (1999): 5–19.

Bullock, Charles S., III, and Ronald Keith Gaddie. "Voting Rights Progress in Georgia." *N.Y.U. Journal of Legislation and Public Policy* 10.1 (2006): 1–49.

Cherny, Robert W. "'No Proven Communist Should Hold a Position at Stanford': Victor Mikhail Arnautoff, the House Un-American Activities Committee, and Stanford." *Sandstone & Tile* 37.3 (2013): 6–7.

Cherny, Robert W. *Victor Arnautoff and the Politics of Art.* Urbana: University of Illinois Press, 2017.

Collins, Patricia Hill. *Fighting Words: Black Women and the Search for Justice.* Minneapolis: University of Minnesota Press, 1998.

Corburn, Jason. "The Discourse of a Community-Based Cumulative Exposure Assessment." *Environmental Management* 29.4 (2002): 451–66.

Cutter, Susan. "Race, Class and Environmental Justice." *Progress in Human Geography* 19.1 (1995): 111–22.

de la Torre, Carlos. "Trump's Populism: Lessons from Latin America." *Postcolonial Studies* 20.2 (2017): 1–12.

Detmer, David. *Sartre Explained: From Bad Faith to Authenticity.* Chicago: Carus, 2008.

Du Bois, W.E.B. *The Souls of Black Folk: Essays and Sketches.* Chicago: A.C. McClurg & Co., 1904.

Du Bois, W.E.B. "The Souls of White Folk" (1920). In *W.E.B. Du Bois: A Reader*, ed. David Levering Lewis. New York: Henry Holt, 1993.

Egerton, Douglas R. *The Wars of Reconstruction: The Brief, Violent History of America's Most Progressive Era.* London: Bloomsbury Press, 2014.

Giambatista, R.C., J.D. Hoover, and L. Tribble. "Millennials, Learning, and Development: Managing Complexity Avoidance and Narcissism." *Psychologist-Manager Journal* 20.3 (2017): 176–93.

Gitin, Maria. *This Bright Light of Ours: Stories from the Voting Rights Fight.* Tuscaloosa: University of Alabama Press, 2014.

Goldwater, Barry. *The Conscience of a Conservative.* Princeton, NJ: Princeton UP, 1960.

Gotanda, Neil. "A Critique of 'Our Constitution Is Color-Blind.'" *Stanford Law Review* 44 (November 1991): 1–68.

Gray, Fred D. *Bus Ride to Justice: Changing the System by the System.* Rev. ed. Montgomery, AL: NewSouth Books, 2013.

Haidt, Jonathan. *The Righteous Mind: Why Good People Are Divided by Politics and Religion.* New York: Pantheon, 2012.

Harwood, S.A. "Environmental Justice on the Streets: Advocacy Planning as a Tool to Contest Environmental Racism." *Journal of Planning Education and Research* 23 (2003): 24–38.

Hasen, Richard L. "Softening Voter ID Laws through Litigation: Is It Enough?" *Wisconsin Law Review*, 20 September 2016.

Holifield, Ryan. "Defining Environmental Justice and Environmental Racism." *Urban Geography* 22.1 (2001): 78–90.

Hollinger, D. "How Wide the Circle of the 'We'? American Intellectuals and the Problem of the Ethnos since World War II." *American Historical Review* 98.2 (1993): 317–37.

Johnson, Samuel. "The Patriot" (1774). In *The Works of Samuel Johnson*, Vol. 14. Troy, NY: Pafraets & Company, 1913. 81–93.

Kelly, Caroline, and Sara Breinlinger. *The Social Psychology of Collective Action: Identity, Injustice and Gender*. Abingdon, UK: Taylor and Francis, 1996.

Landrieu, Mitch. *In the Shadow of Statues: A White Southerner Confronts History*. New York: Viking Press, 2018.

Lehto, Steve. *Death's Door: The Truth Behind the Italian Hall Disaster and the Strike of 1913*. 2nd ed. New York: Momentum, 2013.

McGurty, Eileen. *Transforming Environmentalism*. New Brunswick, NJ: Rutgers University Press, 2007.

McHugh, Nancy. *The Limits of Knowledge: Generating Pragmatist Feminist Cases for Situated Knowing*. Albany: SUNY Press, 2015.

McNamee, Roger. *Zucked: Waking Up to the Facebook Catastrophe*. New York: Penguin, 2019.

Mill, John Stuart. *On Liberty*. London, 1879.

Morgan, Edmund S. *American Slavery, American Freedom: The Ordeal of Colonial Virginia*. New York: W.W. Norton, 1975.

Motta, M. "The Dynamics and Political Implications of Anti-Intellectualism in the United States." *American Politics Research* 46.3 (2017): 465–98.

Nelson, Dana. *Bad for Democracy: How the Presidency Undermines the Power of the People*. Minneapolis: University of Minnesota Press, 2008.

Penrod, Erin A. "Disenfranchisement 2.0: Recent Voter ID Laws and the Implications Thereof." *U. St. Thomas Law Journal* 14.1 (2018): 207–48.

Roediger, David R. *The Wages of Whiteness*. Rev. ed. New York: Verso, 2007.

Rudé, George. *The Crowd in History 1730–1848: A Study of Popular Disturbances in France and England*. London: J.J. Wiley & Sons, 1981.

Sandoval, Chela. *The Methodology of the Oppressed*. Minneapolis: University of Minnesota Press, 2000.

Schecter, Harold. *The Serial Killer Files: The Who, What, Where, How, and Why of the World's Most Terrifying Murderers*. New York: Ballantine Books, 2003.

Siskind, Amy. *The List: A Week-by-Week Reckoning of Trump's First Year*. New York: Bloomsbury, 2018.

Spivak, Gayatri. "Can the Subaltern Speak?" In *Marxism and the Interpretation of Culture*, ed. Cary Nelson and Lawrence Grossberg. London: Macmillan, 1988. 271–315.

Stow, Simon. *American Mourning: Tragedy, Democracy, Resilience*. Cambridge: Cambridge University Press, 2017.

Sullivan, Shannon, and Nancy Tuana, eds. *Race and Epistemologies of Ignorance*. Albany: SUNY Press, 2007.

Tenorio, Julian Santaella, et al. "What Do We Know about the Association between Firearm Legislation and Firearm-Related Injuries?" *Epidemiologic Reviews* 38.1 (2016): 140–57.

Tetlock, P.E. "Cognitive Style and Political Ideology." *Journal of Personality and Social Psychology* 45.1 (1983): 118–26.

Vallotten, C.D., and C. Ayoub. "Symbols Build Communication and Thought: The Role of Gestures and Words in the Development of Engagement Skills and Social-Emotional Concepts during Toddlerhood." *Social Development* 19.2 (2011): 601–26.

Vilanova, F., et al. "Deindividuation: From Le Bon to the Social Identity Model of Deindividuation Effects." *Cogent Psychology* 4.1 (2017): n.p.

Wilkerson, Isabel. *The Warmth of Other Suns*. New York: Vintage, 2010.

Woodward, C. Vann. *Reunion and Reaction: The Compromise of 1877 and the End of Reconstruction*. Boston: Little, Brown & Co., 1966.

Zimring, Carl A. *Clean and White: A History of Environmental Racism in the United States*. New York: New York University Press, 2015.

Zinn, Howard. *A People's History of the United States*. New York: HarperCollins, 2003.

IMAGE CREDITS

From the Publisher

A name never says it all, but the word "Broadview" expresses a good deal of the philosophy behind our company. We are open to a broad range of academic approaches and political viewpoints. We pay attention to the broad impact book publishing and book printing has in the wider world; for some years now we have used 100% recycled paper for most titles. Our publishing program is internationally oriented and broad-ranging. Our individual titles often appeal to a broad readership too; many are of interest as much to general readers as to academics and students.

Founded in 1985, Broadview remains a fully independent company owned by its shareholders—not an imprint or subsidiary of a larger multinational.

For the most accurate information on our books (including information on pricing, editions, and formats) please visit our website at www.broadviewpress.com. Our print books and ebooks are also available for sale on our site.

b

broadview press
www.broadviewpress.com

This book is made of paper from well-managed FSC® - certified
forests, recycled materials, and other controlled sources.